# Sleeping in a Sinking Boat

Finding *peace* in the middle of the storm

TERRY NIGHTINGALE

Ark House Press
arkhousepress.com

Cataloguing in Publication Data:
Title: Sleeping In A Sinking Boat
ISBN: 9781764357715 (pbk)
Subjects: REL099000    RELIGION / Christian Living / Spiritual Warfare; REL023000 RELIGION / Christian Ministry / Discipleship; REL012120    RELIGION / Christian Living / Spiritual Growth.

Design by initiateagency.com

# CONTENTS

# INTRODUCTION

'I am not afraid of the storm because I am learning how to sail my ship.'[1] Laura Dekker became the youngest person to circumnavigate the globe single-handed on 21st Jan 2012. She completed the task in a 40 ft two-masted ketch (named *Guppy*) in 518 days at just 16. She was only 14 years old when she started the journey.

Much has been written about this amazing young lady, but one story stands out. Over a year into her epic journey from Gibraltar, Laura set off from Port Elizabeth heading for Cape Town, South Africa. Not long after her departure, she caught the news from the evening weather forecast that 40 knots of wind were on their way.[2]

Most other boats were turned round at this point to the safety of Port Elizabeth, but Laura remembered similar weather conditions she had faced before and felt no compulsion to follow suit. She was confident of her skills to steer the boat to its destination.

Reaching the point of no return, where there was no shelter, no safe way to return to shore and no place to weigh anchor, Laura entered the storm.

Soon, 40 knots of wind became 65 knots of wind, and the waves heightened rapidly.[3] The boat started taking on water, and Laura had no choice

---

[1] This quote is usually attributed to Louisa Alcott from her book *Little Women*. *Little Women* has little to offer about the skills needed to pilot boats, but it does have something to say about resilience in the face of struggles.
[2] 40 knots is a windspeed of about 46 mph or 74 km/hr
[3] 65 knots is a windspeed of about 75 mph or 120 km/hr

but to keep going, hand-steering the vessel. Braving the severe cold and the long hours, she kept herself focused by repeating, 'one more wave; one more wave; just one more wave ...'

She lived to tell the story but only after many hours with no sleep and her mind and body set to survival mode.[4]

It is amazing what human beings can achieve when their life depends on it.

Franklin D Roosevelt is quoted as saying, 'The only thing we have to fear is fear itself.' He was trying to inspire courage and resilience during the American Great Depression in the late 1920s and early 1930s. The point was that irrational, or even rational fear can paralyse efforts to overcome the problems people face. If Laura had felt any fear, clearly she channelled it into getting the job done.

I wonder how fear affects you. For me, if a work colleague snaps at me for interrupting him, I am probably not going to run away from him. I'll just leave him alone for a while or try a different way of communicating. If I drop a chair on my toe (which happened recently), creating sharp pain and a nice purple bruise, I am not going to become afraid of office furniture. I'll just be more careful next time.

Most of us have a degree of resilience over life's day-by-day stresses and challenges and naturally solve problems as they arise. But when the winds of life suddenly increase from 40 knots to 65 and the threats become more serious, anxiety can easily turn to the type of fear that cripples, and our emotional shields of protection can quickly wear thin. We can become emotionally and rationally paralysed.

Several years ago, I met a man who told me he had once been a victim of a home invasion. He described the incident in some detail, and it became

---

[4]    From the podcast Laura Dekker: storm on the Indian Ocean Podcast Maré Sonora
       - YouTube

clear that the incident had made an indelible mark on him. He had never felt safe since. From that day, every time he found himself in a scenario where even a light confrontation with another was a possibility, he would retreat. Fear had found an open invitation in his heart. In a way he had become the living embodiment of Roosevelt's quote.

This book is an attempt to find out what God says about facing our fears in life's situations and finding peace instead. In a way, it is a reflection of my own journey which, by the way, is far from finished.

I started diving into this topic because of the many times in life and ministry I would feel overwhelmed with that feeling you have in your gut when you are nervous – no, more than nervous – almost panic-stricken about what might lie ahead.

Is that person going to be angry with me again? Will that mistake cost me my job or my position? Will the doctor find something serious when I tell him about those symptoms I am experiencing? Do the people around me know about the things I struggle with? What if they find out the real me?

I don't think Jesus worried about stuff like this and it is not difficult to work out why. He was the Son of God, no less, possessing an infinite connection with his Father in Heaven. He knew his purpose during his short life, he knew the power available to him and he knew the authority he held to speak change.

Jesus wasn't afraid of storms as we will see in the next chapter, but here's the thing: I don't believe we need to be either because he invites us into relationship with him. He invites us into a journey of faith – one where we discover how to walk with the Father through faith in the Son and in the power of the Holy Spirit.

Life is one, big, long, learning process with him.

And maybe learning a journey of faith is a bit like learning to sail a ship. What was that quote again? 'I am not afraid of the storm because I am learning how to sail my ship.' I don't need to be afraid because I am learning how to walk with the Father, through faith in the Son and in the power of the Holy Spirit.

The last time I saw Mel, she was the picture of perfect health. Retirement was looking good on her, she had taken care of herself, and she was enjoying getting more involved in her local church. Six months later came the shock diagnosis: you have stage four lung cancer, and it is inoperable.

The first signs were some rattling sounds in her breathing. Initially the doctors thought she had pneumonia and then long-term pneumonia, before admitting her into hospital for a week. Two months of CT scans, a PET scan, two biopsies and numerous tests followed until eventually the truth came out: she may not have long to live.

She was still waiting for the doctors to decide on a treatment plan when I caught up with her. It was a video chat and, when our phones connected, I was taken aback with the look I saw on her face. She seemed genuinely joyful. Later she wrote to me: 'All through this time God has given me a very strong sense of peace, calm, contentment and joy. The Lord has blessed me with a feeling of "gliding or floating on calm water like a boat on a flat sea".'

If you are looking for peace in the middle of your storm, then maybe this book is for you. Like you, I have many questions, but I believe there are answers. God has given us his Word and he has given us stories of those who have found him to be faithful through the difficult seasons.

# CHAPTER 1

# Two Stories

## ONE (NOT SO FINE) DAY ON THE SEA OF GALILEE

When Jesus saw the crowd around him, he gave orders to cross to the other side of the lake ... Then he got into the boat and his disciples followed him. Suddenly a furious storm came up on the lake, so that the waves swept over the boat. But Jesus was sleeping. The disciples went and woke him, saying, "Lord, save us! We're going to drown!" He replied, "You of little faith, why are you so afraid?" Then he got up and rebuked the winds and the waves, and it was completely calm. The men were amazed and asked, "What kind of man is this? Even the winds and the waves obey him!" (Matthew 8:18, 23–27)

## ONE (NOT SO FINE) DAY ON THE MEDITERRANEAN SEA

The word of the Lord came to Jonah, son of Amittai: "Go to the great city of Nineveh and preach against it, because its wickedness has come up before me." But Jonah ran away from the Lord and headed for Tarshish. He went down to Joppa, where he found a ship bound for that port. After

1

paying the fare, he went aboard and sailed for Tarshish to flee from the Lord.

Then the Lord sent a great wind on the sea, and such a violent storm arose that the ship threatened to break up. All the sailors were afraid, and each cried out to his own god. And they threw the cargo into the sea to lighten the ship.

But Jonah had gone below deck, where he lay down and fell into a deep sleep. The captain went to him and said, "How can you sleep? Get up and call on your god! Maybe he will take notice of us so that we will not perish."

Then the sailors said to each other, "Come, let us cast lots to find out who is responsible for this calamity." They cast lots and the lot fell on Jonah. So, they asked him, "Tell us, who is responsible for making all this trouble for us? What kind of work do you do? Where do you come from? What is your country? From what people are you?"

He answered, "I am a Hebrew, and I worship the Lord, the God of heaven, who made the sea and the dry land." This terrified them and they asked, "What have you done?" (They knew he was running away from the Lord, because he had already told them so.)

The sea was getting rougher and rougher. So, they asked him, "What should we do to you to make the sea calm down for us?"

"Pick me up and throw me into the sea," he replied, "and it will become calm. I know that it is my fault that this great storm has come upon you."

Instead, the men did their best to row back to land. But they could not, for the sea grew even wilder than before. Then they cried out to the Lord, "Please, Lord, do not let us die for taking this man's life. Do not hold us accountable for killing an innocent man, for you, Lord, have done as you pleased." Then they took Jonah and threw him overboard, and the raging sea grew calm. At this the men greatly feared the Lord, and they offered a sacrifice to the Lord and made vows to him (Jonah 1:1–16).

## TWO FURIOUS STORMS. ONE POWERFUL GOD

The three synoptic Gospels (Matthew, Mark and Luke) each carry the extraordinary story of Jesus calming a ferocious storm with a simple word of command. Although we don't know how instant the abatement of the storm was, it was impressive enough for experienced fishermen to huddle together in wonder whispering, "Who is this? Even the wind and the waves obey him!"[5]

And, as we see in the story of Jonah, this isn't the only time that violent winds and waves have been dramatically calmed in a story in the Bible.

When Jonah was on the run from the Lord (because, in his view, that option was preferable to doing what God had asked him to do), he too found himself in wild weather. And like the story recorded in the Gospels, the raging sea and fierce winds fell quickly to a tranquil rest, this time after Jonah was thrown overboard.

Two furious storms. One powerful God.

The God of the Hebrew Scriptures who showed his authority and power over all created things through the story of Jonah, then revealed that same authority and power through his Son, Jesus Christ, by way of a similar miracle. It shouldn't surprise us that Jesus once said, (talking of himself), "… something greater than Jonah is here".[6] No kidding! In fact, someone on the same level as Yahweh, the God of the Old Testament, is here! Jonah commanded the sailors to throw him overboard for God to quell the storm; Jesus commanded the storm itself to be quiet, and it obeyed.

My contention in this book is that these stories are linked. Obviously by Jesus' direct reference to the Old Testament prophet but in other more subtle ways too.

---

[5]   Mark 4:41
[6]   Luke 11:32

3

The same God who breathed all Scripture into being gave us one continuous narrative from Creation to the Book of Revelation.[7] At key points, we hear prophetic voices driving the story forward and we see the Lord carefully moulding history to his will so that promises are kept and predictions come to fulfilment. Jesus himself announced that he had come to fulfil the law and the prophets.[8]

The writers of the New Testament often quoted their Hebrew Scriptures and frequently alluded to their themes either deliberately or obliquely. It is not a new idea that New Testament authors and particularly the Lord Jesus himself drew fresh meaning from the ancient stories of the Old Testament. For example, the writer to the Hebrews taught us that the law in the Torah is merely a shadow of what's to come because Jesus has become ultimate sacrifice.[9] Jesus brought fresh understanding to the Psalms, the Ten Commandments and the utterances of the Prophets[10], before transforming the Passover meal into a powerful commemoration of his forthcoming death on the cross.

So, when we consider the account of Jonah, Jesus invited his hearers to see a connection between them. He drew attention to the prophet on at least two separate occasions, comparing himself directly to him and predicting that his own future will have parallels with Jonah's imprisonment in the belly of a very large fish.[11]

---

[7]  'All Scripture is God-breathed and is useful for teaching, rebuking, correcting and training in righteousness' (2 Timothy 3:16)

[8]  See Matthew 5:17

[9]  Hebrews 10:1-18

[10]  For example, in Matthew 22:44, Jesus challenged the Pharisees' traditional understanding of Psalm 110 and in his 'Sermon on the Mount' he brought new meaning to statements in the Ten Commandments. He explained that murder is now no longer just a physical act, in the Lord's eyes, but the result of anger with intent to harm another.

[11]  See Matthew 12:39-41, 16:4 and Luke 11:29-32

## COMPARING THE TWO STORIES

To visit the two stories involving a storm, the sudden calming of the wind and waves is one obvious similarity between the two, but, if we dive a little deeper, we notice others.

Both Jesus and Jonah were on a mission. They were headed somewhere. They had made an intentional decision to board a boat and they knew where they were going before being interrupted by the storm. Jesus planned to go to the other side of the lake[12], and Jonah was running away to Tarshish. Neither man was aimlessly drifting. Both were focused on their intended destinations. One towards God's purposes, the other against.

The two men were also asleep during the storm before being abruptly woken by others. In each case, those that shook the sleeper were less than happy that he should choose to have a nap at that time, no doubt because everyone else was profoundly frightened of the life and death situation they found themselves in. "Don't you care if we drown?"[13], said the disciples to Jesus. "How can you sleep?"[14], said the sailors to Jonah.

There are also important differences between the two accounts. We have already mentioned that, while we assume Jesus sailed in the direction of His Father's will, Jonah ran the furthest place he could think of to get *away* from God.

Second, while the Lord was the author of the storm bearing down on Jonah (he 'sent a great wind on the sea'), we don't know what brought the bad weather to Jesus' boat. The text gives us no reason for the storm to be there.

---

[12]  Mark 4:35 and Luke 8:22
[13]  Mark 4:38
[14]  Jonah 1:6

Third, Jesus brought an end to the chaos of the swirling winds and angry waves by speaking to them. To the disciples' amazement, the elements obeyed. Although Jonah knew how to bring the storm to an end ("Pick me up and throw me into the sea, and it will become calm"), it was not by his own command or power. The winds and waves died down when his body hit the water. Jonah's solution was to sacrifice himself.

## WHY THE COMPARISON?

Why study these two stories?

As the risen Jesus walked the Emmaus Road, unrecognised by his fellow travellers and hearing their account of his suffering on the cross, Luke tells us that "beginning with Moses and all the Prophets, he explained to them what was said in all the Scriptures concerning himself".[15] Jesus took the opportunity to open up the Old Testament and explain how it points to him.

As already mentioned, Jesus likened himself to Jonah. He described himself as greater. But he said more than that. He said that his very presence on earth at that time and place was a *sign* of Jonah[16], a reference usually taken to parallel Jonah's near-death experience with his own impending death and subsequent resurrection.

"For as Jonah was three days and three nights in the belly of a huge fish, so the Son of Man will be three days and three nights in the heart of the earth."[17]

Just as Jonah was preserved for three days in the belly of a whale and then restored alive to fulfil God's purposes, so also will Jesus accomplish

---

[15] Luke 24:27
[16] Matthew 12:39; 16:4
[17] Matthew 12:40

the Father's purposes. He will die on the day we now call Good Friday, be 'preserved' on Holy Saturday and then be raised to life on the Sunday.

Jesus obeyed his Father, while Jonah disobeyed. Where Jonah found himself at the mercy of a storm sent to steer him back on course, Jesus exercised his authority over it to continue his. Jonah had no choice over his apparent 'death' in the fish and only reluctantly (in my view) completed his task of preaching God's message to the Ninevites. Jesus cleared the storm which had threatened to obstruct his Father's plans, then set his face and will to complete the work the Father had called him to do.

Jesus was the perfect Jonah, the Jonah who got it right. At one with God the Father, Jesus obeyed his Father. He preached God's message, the Good News of the Kingdom of God. Jonah ran in fear from the Ninevites, while Jesus stayed the course.

Jonah probably had some idea of the wickedness that resided in Nineveh, but all he had to do was preach a message of repentance and trust God to take care of him. Although he did the job eventually, his first instinct was to disobey. On the other hand, Jesus submitted his will to the Father's, preached the message of the Kingdom and embraced obedience at its costliest moment – his body and life to the nails of the cross.

If Jesus likened himself to Jonah, then what lessons might we learn from the comparison? If the Father allowed or even placed a storm in the path of Jesus' boat in a way that seems to parallel an event in Jonah's life around 750 years before, then what do these accounts reveal to us? What do they say about human beings? What do they tell us about the purposes of God? And how do they speak to us about our own storms of life?

## PEACE IN THE MIDST OF THE STORM

Which takes us neatly back to the 'why' question: Why bother studying this? Perhaps the best answer is that both stories lead us to contemplate questions about our relationship with God, particularly through tough times. Jesus found peace in the middle of a dangerous weather event and scolded his disciples for not sharing the same calmness of spirit. If Jesus expected the twelve to have more faith, what is he teaching us when our worlds fall apart?

I still remember the day when Janet told us she had been diagnosed with ovarian cancer. Janet was one of three elders in a church I was pastoring. The other two elders and I listened to her relay the news. She described her condition clearly, almost matter-of-factly, before declaring her faith in God, in his power and his sovereignty. We stayed for a while and then prayed with her for healing.

Two years later, I was conducting her funeral, but during the one hour of sadness and celebration, we heard story after story of a lady who had found genuine peace throughout her ordeal. She had even shared the love and truth of Jesus to medical staff along the way.

Janet's storm was not a gentle breeze. There were many times when she asked friends and family for prayer as chemotherapy took its toll and as she faced another day of discomfort and pain. But the light that shone through was faith in the one who could heal in a moment, heal through medical intervention or call her to her heavenly home. She was a peace with whatever option God had for her.

We will come back to her story, and others' later, but let's turn next to the disciples' reaction to a sleeping Jesus amidst a genuinely life-threatening situation. It's not pretty!

## Summary

- The Bible carries two stories involving a boat in a storm and a person sleeping in the middle of it. One is Jesus, the other was the prophet, Jonah.
- Jesus compared his ministry to Jonah's and said that his presence on earth was a sign of Jonah
- Comparing the two stories helps us to contemplate questions about our relationship with God, particularly through tough times.

## Key takeaway

When the storms of life strike, God is more than able to give us peace.

# CHAPTER 2

# *Where is your Faith?*

## LOOK WHO'S IN THE BOAT WITH YOU

Mark tells us that it was evening when they set off from shore and Matthew agrees with that observation.[18] Jesus and his disciples began their journey across the lake after a particularly demanding time of ministry and teaching earlier that afternoon. Jesus was probably grateful for the rest from people.[19] We are told it was Jesus who gave the order to leave, after noting the crowd around him. Mark lets us know that there were other boats making the journey with them.

That afternoon, Jesus would have been teaching whilst sitting in a boat at the water's edge with no indication of impending bad weather. In fact, according to Matthew, when the storm did come, it was sudden and therefore, presumably, unexpected. According to Luke, everyone was in great danger.[20]

And by then the darkness of night would have only amplified everyone's fear.

---

18  See Matthew 8:16
19  As evidenced in verse 18
20  Luke 8:23

Except Jesus.

Boats on the Sea of Galilee were constructed primarily of cedar planks joined together by pegged mortise-and-tenon joints and nails. The boats were shallow with flat bottoms, allowing them to get close to the shore while fishing. The vessels were often made from scrap wood and, over time, might have undergone extensive and repeated fixes, perhaps increasing their vulnerability to strong, pulsating waves. In a violent storm, the loud cracks of creaking joints holding the boat together would have been more than unsettling.

All three storytellers make it clear this was no ordinary weather event; it was a 'furious' squall. The Sea of Galilee was known for its occasional storms, and the Jewish people were a little frightened of the sea – some thought it was full of scary creatures. The turn in the weather in this story, perhaps caused by winds arising from mountains to the north, created powerful gusts and waves tall enough to sweep over the sides of the boats on the lake that day. The disciples must have thought the boats were going to sink leaving little to hold on to.

Jesus was asleep, seemingly oblivious to all this. On a cushion.

In a panic, the disciples woke Jesus with the cry, "Lord, save us!"[21], even though they knew Jesus had little to no experience of sailing vessels and the ocean. Yet clearly, they believed he could, somehow, save them from catastrophe. By then, he had healed and cast out demons, so even though he had not yet shown any authority over the forces of nature, they instinctively knew to look to him for a solution to their predicament.

It might be surprising to us, shocking even, to hear Jesus' reply with "Where is your faith?".[22] Surely, we might protest, they were exercising faith by the mere action of turning to him for help! But a cry of panic is not

---

[21] Matthew 8:25
[22] Luke 8:25

the same as a calm placement of trust. The prophet Isaiah once wrote, "In quietness and trust is your strength".[23] The disciples looked to their master for a solution, but Jesus questioned why their strength had evaporated. If Jesus could quietly and calmly trust Father to sort the situation out, why couldn't they?

In the months before this day, according to Mark's account, Jesus had healed many, including a leper and a paralysed man, cast out evil spirits and amazed people with his teaching. He declared that he was Lord of the Sabbath, and he presumed to declare forgiveness of sins over a paralysed man before healing him. The disciples may not have quite worked out who Jesus was at this point, but they had enough information to tell them he had power beyond any living soul.

If Jesus demonstrated sovereignty over sickness and the forces of evil, then maybe he was sovereign over the forces of nature. "Why are you so afraid? Do you still have no faith?"[24] Open your eyes, disciples, look who is in the boat with you!

## THE STORMS OF LIFE

Life's storms can hit us from any direction. They can be financial, relational, deep in the heart or waging war on our health. Some may come as a result of disobeying God, but more often they are here because our world is in a fallen state, at enmity with God, at the mercy of human decisions and under the influences of demonic powers. They can strike randomly and knock on our door without warning.

'It's not fair,' we might cry, but storms are a part of life and, as we see with both Jonah and Jesus, God is present when they strike. Some storms

---

[23]   Isaiah 30:15
[24]   Mark 4:40

are initiated by the Lord, and some will never betray their origins but as we see in both accounts, God is the solution *in the midst* of them.

Several years ago, a friend of mine, Craig, invited me to join him in speaking at a pastors' conference in Kenya. It was a privilege to accept the invitation, and we spent about eight days there enjoying the first-rate hospitality of the Kenyan people.

We were humbled to be invited back the following year to speak at the same annual conference but unfortunately my friend had other commitments and was not able to attend with me. I didn't want to make the trip alone, so I asked another friend, a brother in Christ with considerable ministry experience on the African continent, Keith, to join me.

Keith kindly accepted but could only attend for three days, so about mid-way through the conference, I was the sole guest left.

The pastors in attendance and my wonderful host made me very welcome and my stay comfortable, but at one point during this visit, something unexpected happened. I felt very homesick; in fact, I had several panic attacks. The feelings were probably exacerbated by problems my wife and I were having trying to reach each other on the phone.

I remember on several occasions, pacing the floor in my hotel room, unable to make contact with friends and family back home and feeling stranded in a country not my own. I was afraid. In my head, it was illogical because my new Kenyan friends were warm, generous and welcoming, but something inside me just snapped. I felt like a lost child; I was desperate to get back to Australia.

I prayed, I prayed, and I prayed again. I wanted to stay and complete my commitments, and I wanted to serve God and the people attending the conference to the best of my ability. I asked God for peace and a calm mind. It felt like there was a storm in my head. Like the disciples, I knew Jesus was the one to turn to but there was no quietness in my soul. No simple trust in God. I knew Jesus *could* calm the storm, but I could find no peace of mind.

Eventually I did get home. I managed to stay long enough to keep my promises but throughout the rest of my time in Kenya, I never reached a place of rest in my heart, despite my prayers that God would do something.

I felt like a failure. There I was, the big shot, important guest speaker, taking a hundred pastors through the Scriptures, while all along, I was a nervous wreck. Promises of Scripture like 'You will keep him in perfect peace, whose mind is stayed on you, because he trusts in you'[25] seemed too far away to grasp.

I had been in a storm, and I had turned to Jesus, but had come to him in a panic, not in quietness and trust. He calmed the storm eventually, but only after I arrived home, and I often wondered why I couldn't deal with the fear I experienced in that hotel room and simply trust Him.

## PERFECT PEACE

Around that time, back in Australia, my wife and I visited a lady in our church. We had heard that Joy was very sick, and the latest diagnosis was not encouraging. We weren't sure what we would say to her as we pressed the doorbell.

She warmly invited us in, and the topic of conversation easily drifted to her health and the likelihood of the doctors finding no more possibilities for her survival. I will never forget the joy matching her name and exuding from her face as she said, 'I have been given my ticket to Heaven and I am going to take it'.

---

[25] Isaiah 26:3, New King James Version

Time could have stopped for us in that moment as we weighed the enormity of our friend's bold and beautiful declaration. I'm sure there must have been moments on her own before that day when the fear and panic of what the cancer was doing to her stirred up a storm in her heart. But, somehow, she had reached a point of leaving the fear behind, looking to Jesus and saying, 'I'm coming home, Lord'.

'You will keep him (or her) in perfect peace, whose mind is stayed on you, because she trusts in you.'

"Where is your faith?" Jesus asked his disciples. The disciples had shown faith by turning to him in the first place, but it was mixed with fear. They didn't turn to Jesus in quietness and trust. "Why are you so afraid?" wondered Jesus. Why listen to fear? Look who's in the boat with you!

## BARRIERS TO FAITH

In my earlier book, *Bite-size Devotions for the Busy Christian*, I wrote a devotion called 'Barriers to faith'.[26] In a nutshell, it described how Jesus once made an extraordinary statement about the *amount* of faith needed to see some kind of change occurring in a person's life.

"If you have faith as small as a mustard seed, you can say to this mountain, 'Move from here to there', and it will move. Nothing will be impossible for you."[27] For Jesus, just a tiny amount of faith in him is all we need. So, in the devotion I asked: what do we do when we don't feel have enough?

We looked at the story of a father of a demon-possessed boy in Mark 9. He came to Jesus and said, "If you can do anything, take pity on us and help us." Jesus took issue with the father's first three words. "If you can?" he

---

[26] Published with *Kharis Publishing*, 2021
[27] Matthew 17:20

replied, "Everything is possible for those who believe." And then the father gave that famous response, "I do believe; help me overcome my unbelief!"[28]

Without realising it, the father had identified something very important: 'I do believe (I have mustard seed faith), but please help me overcome my unbelief (help me overcome the thing that is getting in the way of my faith).'

We also looked at the story of Jairus. Jairus was a synagogue ruler who came to Jesus and pleaded with him to heal his very sick daughter.[29] Jesus indicated to him that he would go to his house and minister to her, but they were interrupted. By the time they reached the house, the girl was dead.

It would have been so easy for Jairus to give up at this point. The facts were clear – it was too late, and the girl had died. But Jesus said, "Don't be afraid; just believe."[30]

This time Jesus confronted both major barriers to faith – fear and facts; or rather, doubts because of facts. Jesus wasn't asking Jairus to ignore the facts and he wasn't asking him to try to psych up more faith. He was simply saying, 'Look at me' – 'look beyond the facts and the fear and believe in me'.

One illustration I have found helpful is to imagine a dirty window. You can still see though it to the view beyond, but the pane of glass is covered with dirt and grime. It would be easy to focus our eyes on the job before us that shouts, 'Please clean me!'. To look only at the grime clinging to the glass.

But now let's picture a beautiful sunrise occurring in the distance and, if we could for a moment, take our eyes off the annoying mess on the window

---

[28] Mark 9:24
[29] Mark 5:22
[30] Mark 5:36

and look at the spectacular array of colours as the sky catches fire, announcing that a new day has come. In other words, if we can peer *through* the dirt that is trying to hold our attention and instead focus on the glory beyond, then we might see past the immediate and gaze at the eternal.

I think that's what Joy discovered. The ability to look beyond the fear and the doubt and see Jesus. Perhaps that's what Jesus expected of his disciples: to somehow look beyond the fact that their boat was about to fall apart and refocus their eyes on the one who had demonstrated authority over both the natural and the supernatural. The one who was so unstressed about the situation that he could even take a nap!

When Jesus asked, 'Where is your faith?', perhaps what he was really asking was, 'Why are you only looking at the storm and the sinking boat? Why are you focused on the wind and waves and believing the worst? Why submit to fear when you can look at me?' Perhaps Jesus hoped they might remember their Old Testament Psalms, especially Psalm 23, where David writes, 'Even though I walk through the valley of the shadow of death, I will fear no evil, for you are with me'.[31]

Is this possible? Can we really apply this to our lives?

## A PLACE NEAR YOUR ALTAR

Like most people, I was shocked when the COVID-19 virus first hit the shores of my country. Up until then, it had been 'foreign' news. However, the time between the first reported cases and an alarming surge was only a matter of a few weeks - 15 cases in the middle of February 2020 to over 400 in mid-March. By the end of March, the numbers had risen to 5,000

---

[31]  Psalm 23:4 (English Standard Version)

across Australia. The reported cases kept going up and up. It was worse, of course, in countless other places across the globe.

Like many of us I remember the day we were called into our first lockdown. Sitting in my bedclothes after watching the news on TV, I retreated into my lounge and felt panic come over me. The same type of anxious feelings I had experienced all those years ago in Kenya.

I picked up my Bible and started praying for something to help me focus on God. As a pastor, I wanted to be a help to people, not a nervous wreck!

I can't remember why, but I started reading Psalm 84:

> How lovely is your dwelling place, Lord Almighty!
> My soul yearns, even faints, for the courts of the Lord.

Yes, that is what I wanted. The courts of the Lord, his presence, but how could I find that place of peace and trust? It was only then that I noticed the verse about sparrows and swallows:

> Even the sparrow has found a home, and the swallow a nest
> for herself,
> where she may have her young — a place near your altar,
> Lord Almighty, my King and my God.[32]

To be honest, I'd always skipped over this part of the psalm. It was rather quaint, I thought, a pleasant picture of a few random birds fluttering around the temple, but something hit me that I had never seen before.

Even birds, who, as far as we know, have no concept of God or his presence, have chosen to build their nest, their home as near as possible to the altar of the temple. Their home-base from where they come and go, where

---

[32] Psalm 84:3

they rest, and where they feed their young is as close to the presence of God as they can be.

The swallow and sparrow don't just fly past the holy place every now and then, or even perch there occasionally. They have set up shop there. They are living there.

I think God was saying to me that if I am to make any dent on my enemy, fear, it was time I started to build my nest in his presence. My heart and mind needed to learn how to live in his proximity. Not just turn up now and then. It is not enough to be there on Sundays, or pop-in occasionally, there is a dwelling that needs to take place. Daily. More than daily. Throughout the day.

Perhaps that is why Jesus asked his disciples where their faith was. They had lived with him for some time. They had literally dwelt with him. They had known the daily peace of His company, and that day he was with them in the boat.

Maybe there is more to be gleaned in these two stories about dwelling in the Lord's presence. For the next chapter, we will go back in time. Why did Jesus and Jonah make their respective trips in the first place and why is that important?

## Summary

- Noticing the disciples' fear of the storm and their predicament, Jesus asked them 'Where is your faith?'.
- Jesus had previously demonstrated his sovereignty over sickness and the forces of evil.
- If we are honest, we can turn to Jesus in times of crises, like the disciples did, but without finding a place of calm and trust.

- When Jesus asks, "Where is your faith?", perhaps what he is really saying is 'It's ok, stop staring at the grime on the window. Look past it, beyond the fear and doubt, and fix your gaze on me'.

## Key takeaway

When the storms of life strike, remember who is in the boat with you.

# CHAPTER 3

# Let's go to the other side

"Where there is no vision, the people perish", says the well-known proverb.[33] Scriptures like this are often used to encourage Christian businesses and organisations, including churches, towards having a clear picture of where they are headed in terms of goals and strategies.

It should be said though that the second half of the verse is often missed out: "… but happy is he who keeps the law."[34] Actually, the phrase, 'the people perish' can also be translated, 'the people cast off restraint'. In other words, the whole verse is about the revelation of God through his law and that, when people abandon God's Word, when there is no preaching of God's Word or prophetic vision, then the people 'cast off restraint' and go their own way.

Putting all that together, any person or organisation would be wise to seek God's will and strategy for them within the overall context of his Word. Most leaders would agree that, when there is no clear vision in an organisation, a lot of effort might be spent with only meagre results. To take that further, when plans don't align with God's Word, can we really

---

33 Proverbs 29:18a
34 In verse 18b

expect His blessings? Both the framework of Holy Scripture and a clear sense of his leading are needed.

## A CLEAR VISION FORWARD

Jesus always knew where he was going. We can deduce this from two pieces of evidence. First, he knew, ultimately, that he was headed for the cross. On at least six occasions he told his disciples something like this:

> We are going up to Jerusalem, and the Son of Man will be delivered over to the chief priests and the teachers of the law. They will condemn him to death and will hand him over to the Gentiles, who will mock him and spit on him, flog him and kill him. Three days later he will rise.[35]

In other words, Jesus always saw the bigger picture. He knew his Father's will; he knew God's Word. He would minister in various places throughout the nation of Israel and beyond, but ultimately the trail would end in Jerusalem and death on the cross. Jesus knew that from the beginning. He did not come to planet Earth to be served, 'but to serve, and to give his life as a ransom for many'.[36] Jesus had a strong sense of purpose.

But we can also infer that Jesus had a pretty good grasp of the Father's short-term, daily and even moment-by-moment plans during his three-year ministry. As we said in the Introduction, Jesus did what he saw the Father doing. One way of discovering the Father's will would likely have been through direct communication during his frequent times of prayer. There are several references in the gospels to Jesus finding a secluded place

---

[35] Mark 10:33–34
[36] Matthew 20:28

to pray.[37] Sometimes a place in the wilderness, other times away from the bustle of life on the side of a mountain. Luke tells us this happened often.[38]

Have you ever wondered what Jesus prayed about? The Scriptures allow us to witness his intense prayers in Gethsemane just before his arrest, and occasionally we hear words to his Father in the presence of his disciples when he blessed children[39] or when he performed a miracle[40], but we know little of the content of his prayers when he was alone with His Father.

There are, however, a couple of references that might help. Before the raising of Lazarus from the dead, Jesus thanked the Father that he always heard his prayers[41], and we know that he could equally discern the Father's voice as shown by the Father's response in the next chapter: "Father, glorify your name!" Then a voice came from heaven, "I have glorified it, and will glorify it again".[42]

We must surely therefore expect an ease of communication between Father and Son even though Jesus is not yet in his ascended form. So, when Jesus said, 'Let's go to the other side', we can surmise that this unlikely to be a whim on his part, or a desire for a pleasant boat trip. It wasn't just a good idea at the time. This was a confident step into his heavenly Father's next plans for the day, discerned through fellowship, prayer and listening to his voice. We are going to the other side because that's what the Father wants us to do.

---

[37]　For example, in Mark 1:35
[38]　See Luke 5:16
[39]　For example, in Matthew 19:13
[40]　E.g. Mark 6:41
[41]　John 11:41
[42]　John 12:28

## KNOWING WHERE YOU ARE GOING

Jonah's resolution to take a sea trip held equal determination, but he didn't arrive at that decision through communion with God. In fact, after the command to go to Nineveh and preach to Israel's enemies, he probably never wanted to hear God's voice again. Jonah made up his mind to escape to the other side of the Mediterranean Sea and hide in a hole somewhere. He will run from the Lord's call upon His life if it's the last thing he does. Jonah knew what he was doing, and, like Jesus, he knew his destination. He would head for Tarshish, a really long way away.

Jesus with his disciples, and Jonah and his shipmates set sail, without knowledge of the impending catastrophic change in the weather. When it came, the storm rocked their vessels and threatened their lives, but it also laid bare their hearts. The disciples were terrified, and Jonah's crew were equally terrified. Jonah resigned himself to God's judgment (which in his mind probably meant death), and Jesus lay quietly asleep on a cushion.

Jesus seemed completely unconcerned as his boat took on water. He was at peace. As we have suggested, perhaps he was confident that his command to 'go to the other side' was more than just an impulse or an idea. It was the Father's will. Therefore, it will happen, regardless of the little distraction of destructive winds and pounding waves.

Even Jonah seemed unshaken by the storm. He calmly instructed the sailors to throw him overboard, knowing that would end the crisis for them. Either he figured the Lord's judgment for him was death by drowning, or he may have contemplated the slim chance of a divine rescue. Whichever way, Jonah knew that God had caught up with him because he had no doubt the sea would become miraculously calm as soon as he hit the water.[43] Jonah

---

[43] See Jonah 1:12

still had a destination in mind although now a revised one: death or deliverance into the hands of the God he had brazenly disobeyed.

Jesus expected life to continue beyond the storm because the Father was with him, and his purposes would be fulfilled. Jonah likely expected death or an uncomfortable rescue. If it is rescue, it will be to obey the Lord's original instructions to him, which in his mind may have been death anyway through the hands of the Ninevites. Both Jesus and Jonah knew that the rest of the day was in the hands of God. For obvious reasons, Jesus was the one experiencing genuine peace.

Perhaps that is part of the hope that God provides in the midst of the storms of life: to know something of where we are going in the greater purposes of God. To be certain that the storm will pass because God's will is infinitely bigger. To know that a journey will continue because he willed it, and it is in his hands.

## UNLESS THE LORD BUILDS THE HOUSE

One church I was involved with didn't employ a pastor until several years after its launch. Then, when the first pastor was appointed, there were a string of difficulties to deal with. There was division among some members, resulting in several people leaving the church. After three further years, the first pastor felt that it was time to move on and I found myself serving as the second.

At that time, there were a handful of families with children and teens and a few young adults. There were some retired couples and a few elderly people. Approximately 50–60 people attended the Sunday services, and a good proportion participated in a mid-week Bible study. At least at first.

Slowly, over time, more people moved on, and I couldn't work out what was happening. Some simply stopped going to church altogether; some transferred to churches with bigger and better programs. If a few new families and individuals had not joined the church during that time, the congregation would have shrunk to a level where the ministry would have become unsustainable. Three years after I arrived, the church was almost half the size it was the first day I preached there. I seriously wondered if I was the right man for the job!

I concluded that, if ever there was a season to have confidence in the destination God had for us, it was now. But there was no clear vision of that destination. My leadership team and I had to admit that, although the church's stated values were sound, there had never really been a clear, engaging call that would energise the people of God towards an attainable goal in God's purposes.

If a visitor to our church had asked any regular attender what the church's stated vision was – what the church was aiming to achieve in our corner of the world – they probably would not have known how to answer. It had taken me three years to realise this.

And, even worse, without that vision and call from God to build the ministry he had for us, when more and more people left, when the boat began to sink, I found it all too easy to believe that an end to the church's life was not far away.

So, my co-leaders and I literally went back into the classroom. We sat in the science lab of a high school and started asking some basic questions. What has God called us to do? What resonates in all of our hearts as to our reason for the church's existence in this part of our city? What is our current church culture? What will it need to become to achieve our vision? What is the Father saying to us? In other words, what do we need to communicate to our people and how do we start edging closer to the vision?

Earlier in the year during a personal time of prayer I had felt God impress something important on my heart. I had spent a lot of time and energy up to that point looking for people who might join the church and boost the numbers, so that there would be more hands on deck for all the busy work of running a local church and, in particular, weekly services on a Sunday.

Some people helped us out for a while, but very few of those I asked were able to make long-term commitments. It was then that something in the Scriptures hit me. In Psalm 127, the psalmist writes:

> Unless the Lord builds the house,
> the builders labour in vain.
> Unless the Lord watches over the city,
> the guards stand watch in vain.[44]

Jesus said something similar, following a significant day in Simon Peter's life. Referring to Peter's faith and declaration that his master was the Christ, the Son of the Living God, Jesus replied with, "Blessed are you, Simon, son of Jonah, for this was not revealed to you by flesh and blood, but by my Father in heaven. And I tell you that you are Peter, and on this rock, I will build my church …"[45]

"I will build my church", said Jesus. Some commentators believe Jesus was making a deliberate allusion to the verses in Psalm 127 above. In other words, ultimately it is the Lord's responsibility to build his house. It is his kingdom and his church. He is the one who builds the church, not me.

So, what were *we* called to do? Jesus made that clear too with probably the last thing he said to his disciples before he left the earth:

> All authority in heaven and on earth has been given to me.
> Therefore, go and make disciples of all nations, baptizing

---

[44] Psalm 127:1
[45] Matthew 16:17

them in the name of the Father and of the Son and of the Holy Spirit, and teaching them to obey everything I have commanded you. And surely, I am with you always, to the very end of the age.[46]

Many have preached and written about this, but I hadn't seen it before. Ultimately, it is not my responsibility to build the church. It is not my fellow leaders' responsibility to build the church. Our responsibility is simply to go out of our four walls and into our neighbourhoods and make disciples.

Of course, we do engage in things that are church-building activities, but what I needed to see was that God holds all of that in his very capable hands and that our focus needed to be the gospel and the making of disciples.

This helped my team and me to realise our vision and it wasn't long before we started forming a new vision statement. Despite our few numbers and need for more resources and expertise, we would trust God for his provision and make no apology that we exist to reach the 'lost' in our local area.

Eventually, our new church vision in terms of a statement became, 'We are called to adventure, a journey to engage with the local community, sharing the love of God and the gospel of Jesus Christ, making disciples of all nations'. Now, despite the storm of shrinking numbers, we could rest in the boat of God's purposes, knowing more clearly where our destination was.

Jesus had said to his disciples, 'Let's go to the other side'. He knew where he was leading them. It was time for us to say the same thing. Let's go to the other side of these walls, beyond the room we meet in for our weekly

---

[46] Matthew 28:18-19

gatherings. Let's declare clearly that we are here for the unsaved and form our strategies around that.

If we were going to weather the storm of a shrinking congregation, with fewer people doing more work, and potentially less money to support the work; if the boat felt, at times, that we might be close to sinking, then we just needed to hold on to our belief that God had called us to a clear purpose – we were going on mission to the people of our neighbourhood with the love of God and the gospel of Jesus Christ.

Years later, and long after it was time for me to move on, the church is still serving God towards the same destination. Their vision and mission to reach out to the local community has since grown to include new and fresh ideas, including a fruitful collaboration with another nearby church. Many people have since heard the gospel, new people have joined the work, and storms have not destroyed it.

So, is it as easy as that? Know where God is leading you and that will help you find the peace you need.

## PEACE THROUGH A NEW DIRECTION

That was certainly true at another time in my life when I was feeling increasingly uneasy about a job I was being paid to do. Although I had been in the organisation for some time, and I believed in the virtue of persevering when circumstances are tough, I had a growing sense that God was telling me my time at the place was up. He had other things he wanted me to do. I had an idea of the kind of thing God wanted me to do, but no details at that point.

So, without a job to step into, I handed in my notice and a huge sense of peace came over me. Over the next few months, I knew the decisions

I needed to make, I had several conversations with different people and eventually I was offered a new job, which I accepted.

God gave me peace when I realised and stepped into the new direction he was calling me. God gave me peace when I focused my thoughts on his calling on my life and how he wants to use my gifts and abilities.

The trouble is, we may know where we are going, we may have some idea of the things God wants us to do, but then new challenges come. New directions steer us towards different situations and people. Some may be a great blessing, but some may not. Knowing our long-term or short-term calling as children of God may be helpful, but that doesn't stop the storms from blowing in.

So, how can we sleep in peace like Jesus at such times? Or even every time? We will look at that soon, but first let's join Jonah on his boat to Tarshish.

## Summary

- Jesus knew where he was going, ultimately to the cross. Throughout his ministry, he did what he saw the Father doing.
- He had a clear sense of purpose and regularly sought the Father's leading through prayer.
- Jesus was at peace in the boat because he was confident that he and disciples would 'go to the other side', regardless of the interruption of the storm.

## Key takeaway

When the storms of life strike, we can sometimes find peace when we have clarity about God's plans and purposes for us.

# CHAPTER 4

## *The sleep of sorrow*

### SLEEPING THROUGH THE NOISE

When we compare the stories of Jesus and Jonah, it is interesting to note that both fell asleep in the middle of a loud and confronting storm. Not just Jesus. Had Jonah found a place of peace as well, despite his disobedience?

Many years ago, when we were first married, Sue and I lived in a ground floor flat (apartment) in a small town in the UK. During one memorable night, there was a storm. It has since been called The Great Storm of 1987, an extratropical cyclone that occurred on 15th-16th October. Hurricane force winds tore across Northern France, the south of England and the English Channel. We lived an hour's drive south of London.

On the morning of the 16th, forests, parks, gardens and roads were overwhelmed with fallen trees. Schools were closed, and many buildings were left without power. At least 22 people lost their lives. The local and national weather reports the previous day had failed to predict the severity of the oncoming change in the weather. One BBC reporter supposedly labelled the approaching storm as a false alarm, becoming one of British TV's 'classic gaffes'.

Sue and I slept through the whole thing! The first indication that there was something wrong was when we opened our front door in the morning to get into the car and go to work - our porch was strewn with contents of an upturned rubbish bin.

Convinced it was 'kids' playing a joke on us, we quickly cleared up the mess and headed off in the car. To our surprise, the road leading out of our small town was blocked with a tree lying on its side. We turned around and pursued an alternate route. That too was obstructed with large, broken branches and another fallen tree.

When it became clear that a storm had hit us overnight, we turned on the car radio and realised what we had missed – what we had slept through.

I don't think we would have fallen asleep through the kind of storms striking the boats of Jonah and Jesus. To a certain extent, Sue and I had been shielded from the danger (and kept from hearing it) by solid brick walls and a situation in town where we were flanked by other sturdy and taller buildings. We were not nearly as vulnerable as a wooden boat on a rough, choppy sea.

## AVOIDING REALITY

Looking closely at the text of the book of Jonah, we note that he fell into a *deep* sleep through his storm. Other translations say he fell fast asleep. The term 'sound asleep' could also have been used, but all mean that Jonah was in a state of being difficult to wake. Does that mean he was at peace?

Some believe he was, in fact, in a tranquil state because, up to that point, he believed he had successfully run from God. He had won; he was far from God and would no longer be required to preach to those terrible Ninevites. On the other hand, others suggest that he was in the 'sleep of sorrow'[47], the desire to escape reality through sleep, even if just for a couple of minutes.

So, was Jonah in a state of peace, or was his sleep a deliberate attempt to avoid facing the stress of his immediate situation – a sleep of escape, an escape from reality?

It is my belief that Jonah knew the seriousness of his decision and he likely felt the weight of it. Guilt is a powerful emotion as we see in Psalm 32 below, words which remind us that those in relationship with God cannot find peace while they cling to unconfessed sin.

> When I kept silent,
> my bones wasted away
> through my groaning all day long.
> For day and night
> your hand was heavy on me;
> my strength was sapped
> as in the heat of summer.
>
> Then I acknowledged my sin to you
> and did not cover up my iniquity.
> I said, "I will confess
> my transgressions to the LORD."
> And you forgave
> the guilt of my sin".[48]

---

[47] For example, in *The Prodigal Prophet*, p33. Tim Keller quoting Scottish minister Hugh Martin.

[48] Psalm 32:3–5

God had been very clear regarding his instructions to Jonah: 'Go to the great city of Nineveh and preach against it, because its wickedness has come up before me'.[49] Jonah was equally clear in his refusal to comply.

It is difficult to imagine a man who knew how to recognise the word of the Lord not feeling any guilt and not experiencing fear after so brazenly disobeying him. It seems more likely that his desire was as much to run away from God's voice as it was from the repercussions of his own actions. Perhaps part of him imagined or realised that the worsening storm assaulting the boat he was hiding on was God finally catching up with him. By falling into a deep sleep, he could literally close his eyes to the inevitable, even if only for a few moments.

According to some psychologists today, human beings sometimes choose sleep over facing a threat or a difficult decision. If I have difficult thoughts or feelings or if I am feeling unusually anxious, I might hope that sleep will take all of it away. It is certainly one way to force a sort of temporary peace, and it is an understandable coping mechanism, but is it the sort of peace God wants to give us?

The trouble with hiding away, shutting our eyes to avoid the stress or pain, is that the peace we find is only temporary, and the situation that caused the anxiety remains unresolved. We have to wake up sometime, and the threat will still be knocking at the door.

## GOD WITH US IN OUR ANXIETY

Common knowledge suggests a plethora of healthy ways of coping with anxiety or fear, like relaxation, natural diets, exercise, affirming relation-

---

[49] Jonah 1:2

ships and support from loved ones.[50] But I wonder if there is anything in the Scriptures that might help. Jesus once said that the peace he gives is not the same as that offered by the world[51], so what hope can we find in the pages of the Bible?

First, there are numerous encouragements to not worry or not be anxious. Here's one of the more well-known ones: 'Do not be anxious about anything, but in every situation, by prayer and petition, with thanksgiving, present your requests to God. And the peace of God, which transcends all understanding, will guard your hearts and your minds in Christ Jesus'.[52]

This is a promise of Scripture. An incredible promise, but it can also be used carelessly. If we just recite these words glibly or toss them out to a struggling friend as a platitude, without careful thought, the words may lose their power.

The author, Paul, knew what it was to be in fear and to regularly face anxiety. On his ministry journeys, we read about him facing dangers, persecution and hardship. Sometimes without letup. When he first arrived in Corinth, he was literally shaking with fear.[53] He cannot therefore be expecting his readers never to feel fear or anxiety. Perhaps his exhortation is to not remain there unchecked but move as soon as possible to prayer.

But it is not a simple 'Just pray, and it will be ok'. Like the birds in the temple dwelling in God's presence, Paul is trying to be *with* God as much as possible. He wants to pray in every situation and about every situation with different types of prayers, clearly outlining his needs and not forget-

---

50  One author I came across even suggested a sort of self 'pep-talk' might be helpful to some. Something that might begin with, 'come on me, you can't avoid this situation, and you can't deny the anxieties that you feel about it, but you can make some small, intentional steps towards...'etc

51  See John 14:27

52  Philippians 4:6-7

53  "I came to you in weakness with great fear and trembling." (1 Corinthians 2:3)

ting to be thankful. In that relationship with the Lord, he finds peace. And he believes his readers will too if they do the same things.

The Bible also tells us we can speak truth, declare it with our lips. "The Lord is my helper; I will not be afraid" writes the author of Hebrews[54]. The Bible has a lot to say about speaking out God's Word, declaring it to those around us, to the Lord, to the principalities and powers and to our own hearts.

Paul quoted from Deuteronomy, "The word is near you; it is in your mouth and in your heart"[55] while the psalmist declared, "My mouth will speak words of wisdom".[56] I know for me something happens in my mind and my heart when I read God's Word out loud. When I read it slowly and let it settle in my spirit.

When we are tempted to sleep (or anything else) as a way of avoiding pain or stress, perhaps the most powerful help is the simple reminder that God is with us. Jesus is in the boat with us, and we can pray to him. We can declare the truth of his promises and commit our situations to him with thanksgiving.

## REPENTANCE AND RESTORATION

However, as we know, the most obvious difference between Jonah in the storm and Jesus in his storm is that Jesus lived in perfect, intimate relationship with his Father, while Jonah did not want his God anywhere near him. Jonah was in no mood to speak God's Word or pray to him. God needed to bring him to a point of repentance. Jonah needed his relationship with God to be restored.

---

[54] Hebrews 13:6
[55] Romans 10:8, quoting from Deuteronomy 30: 14
[56] Psalm 49:3

The language of Jonah's prayer in the second chapter of his book reveals a powerful contrast between a man trying to avoid God as in the first chapter with a man wanting communion with him a short time later. A wonderful example of the mercy of God. Through the unusual and rather unexpected introduction of a large fish to the story, Jonah found the heart to repent of his actions. And he seems almost surprised that God would want fellowship with him after his initial decision to disobey.

> In my distress I called to the LORD,
> and he answered me.
> From deep in the realm of the dead I called for help,
> and you listened to my cry.[57]

> To the roots of the mountains I sank down;
> the earth beneath barred me in forever.
> But you, LORD my God,
> brought my life up from the pit.[58]

I was desperate, Jonah recalls, and called out to the Lord, and he answered me. I was as good as dead, but the Lord heard my cries for help. I had no hope of rescue but you, Lord, personally brought me up from the pit. God didn't just rescue Jonah from drowning. He restored their relationship.

The Lord had once said to another Old Testament character, Joshua, 'Do not be afraid; do not be discouraged, for the Lord your God will be with you wherever you go'.[59] The Lord's encouragement to Joshua, as Joshua prepared himself for the biggest challenge of his life – to lead his people into countless bloody battles – was to command him not to be

---

[57]  Jonah 2:2
[58]  Jonah 2:6
[59]  Joshua 1:9

afraid or discouraged. And he backed it up with one promise that made all the difference: The Lord is with you.

Jonah said that the Lord answered him in his distress. I wonder if the Lord said something like 'I am with you', an assurance that their relationship was restored. We don't know, but Jonah's prayer reveals a heart grateful to be saved from death and back in fellowship with God.

If we turn to the sleep of sorrow, or any other coping mechanism to take our minds off the storm or the reasons behind the storm, perhaps some hard questions need to be asked: Are we running away from the Lord's will in our lives? Are we fleeing the consequences of disobedience? Do we need to return to fellowship with the Lord?

We don't need the sleep of sorrow, sleep as a way of escape, once we realise who is with us and how he might want us to move forward in obedience to him.

Perhaps you have been running away from the Lord for some time or resisting his will. Perhaps your relationship with the Father has suffered some damage as a result. You have tried to fill the void of his absence with a variety of coping mechanisms, but, in the end, you know there is only one decision to make: you need to return to your maker.

Jonah's biggest need was not to be rescued from rough seas; it was to be restored into relationship with his God. His greatest need was to know, once again, that the Lord was with him. To see that God had not abandoned him, even though he had tried to hide from him. He needed to submit to God being in charge again.

Running from God may not always look as dramatic as a ship to the opposite end of the sea. It might be a second glance or a slow walk towards temptation. It might be a wilful reluctance to listen to wise advice. It might be a choice to hang on to unforgiveness. Worse, it might be a destructive relationship or questionable business decision. But when we run from the will of God, we cannot escape from him. His love pursues us until we repent.

And perhaps that is the point. Jesus, in contrast to Jonah, knew the love of the Father, even to the cross. If Jonah had truly understood the depths of God's love for him (and God's love, even for the Ninevites), maybe that account of history would have been recorded differently.

I remember, as a young man and new Christian, fearing that God might call me to do something I really didn't want to do. Like Jonah being told to go to a notoriously violent people and preach there. What if he was telling me to go and be a missionary in some far-off place that was dangerous, somewhere where I might be lonely or unsafe? What if he was telling me literally to give up everything?

The truth is, God does call many of his children to difficult ministries and circumstances, but for those who are able to trust in his constant love and presence, he equips and sustains them.

In hindsight, I think I knew intellectually that God had made me and that Jesus had died on a cross for me, but I hadn't yet begun to grasp the infinite depths of his sacrificial love for me. Perhaps it was a similar story for Jonah. He knew God was real and he had experienced God speaking to him and through him. But did he fully understand God's love and what it means for God to be with him?

## Summary

- Jonah's sleep was likely a 'sleep of sorrow', an attempt to escape from the consequences of his disobedience to God's command to go to Nineveh.
- Turning to the Lord in prayer through difficult times can bring us to peace, as can declaring the truth of God's Word and his promises.

- Jonah's need was to welcome God's presence instead of running away from him. He needed to repent of his sin.

## Key takeaway

When storms of life strike, repentance may be the key to bringing us the peace we are looking for.

# CHAPTER 5

## *The sleep of peace*

While Jonah slept in an attempt to flee from his fears, Jesus put his head down in a storm without any fear. The wind and waves threatening the small group of boats, likely piloted by some of his own disciples, that is, experienced fishermen, struck the flotilla with such force that all but the Saviour were convinced they were about to drown.

Sailors, who knew the changing nature of the sea, would have recognised the threats unfolding before them: ominous dark clouds stealing the light, gusts of wind increasing with intensity and waves that were sweeping over the edge of the wooden crafts, filling the hulls, each one in danger of being completely swamped.[60] At some point in the journey, the disciples must have realised they had entered a world usually frequented only through campfire stories and legends.

According to Luke, Jesus had fallen asleep before the weather changed. We can imagine at that time the calm rocking motion of the vessel and a soft cushion giving him the perfect opportunity to rest after a busy time of ministry.[61] But was he aware of the storm as it closed in?

---

60   See Matthew 8:24
61   See Mark 4:38

Certainly, he seems unsurprised by the situation and quite unconcerned. As we noted in Chapter Two, according to Matthew's account, the first thing he says upon waking is, 'You of little faith, why are you so afraid?'. One suggestion is that Jesus had in fact been dozing, sleeping lightly and fully aware of the circumstances around him. However, unlike Jonah, he wasn't shutting his eyes to try to escape from reality. And he wasn't afraid. He was simply at peace. He knew everything was going to be ok.

How could Jesus have remained so calm during this frightening episode?

## KEEPING CALM

Most of us have met people who seem to be able to sail through life's stormy circumstances, holding it together with unruffled tranquillity, despite the voices of panic around them. I remember one time on holiday, helping a family trying to rescue their collapsing tent in the middle of a heavy downpour of rain. While the husband frantically pulled on guy ropes and hammered in tent pegs, his wife, a mum of five boys (who were outside enjoying the puddles), patiently held the canvas to one of the poles. Smiling serenely, her quiet composure seemed almost unreal.

But not everybody is blessed to have such a personality. And of course, most people who project the appearance of a white swan gently gliding down the river are adept at hiding their legs under the water as they paddle like there's no tomorrow. A calm exterior doesn't always guarantee a peaceful interior.

On the other hand, the tone of Jesus' response to his panic-stricken friends does suggest a soul at ease, despite the chaos around him. When Jesus says to those who have woken him up, "You of little faith, why are you so afraid?", probably as he is slowly getting to his feet, it feels to me a response a bit like, 'Everything is ok. Relax! Why are you so stressed?'.

Why was Jesus so seemingly unaffected by the dangers and panic around him? Perhaps it had to do with his deep connection with God the Father. If we take a closer look at Jesus' relationship with his Father, we might see clues that help us understand his peace in such a stressful situation. A good place to start is in the Gospel of John, where we find many verses linking Jesus with his Father in Heaven.

## THE LOVE OF FATHER AND SON

John the disciple introduces us to Jesus and the Father right at the beginning of his gospel. 'No one has ever seen God, but the one and only Son, who is himself God and is in closest relationship with the Father, has made him known.'[62] John, who many argue was 'the disciple whom Jesus loved'[63], observed from close quarters the even deeper love shared by Father and Son.

Likewise, another John, John the Baptist, also drew attention to the love shared by two of the three members of the Godhead: "The Father loves the Son and has placed everything in his hands."[64] His comment about placing everything in his hands is likely a reference to Jesus' role as mediator between God the Father and sinful humanity, combined with the authority to speak to humans as God incarnate, heal the sick and deliver people from evil spirits. According to John the Baptist, Jesus had a job to do, and he was fully commissioned and equipped by the Father to do it.

From Jesus' perspective, he and his Father worked together in close partnership. Speaking to Jewish leaders who were criticising him for doing what they considered unlawful on the Sabbath, he said, "My Father is always at

---

[62] John 1:18
[63] John 13:23
[64] John 3:35

his work to this very day, and I too am working."[65] It goes without saying that most of the religious elite were extremely uncomfortable in the way that he referred to the Father. At one time, he even went as far as saying, "I and the Father are one"[66] to angry religious leaders – how dare he suggest that they are equal![67]

According to Jesus, the Father entrusted all matters of judgment to him[68] and granted him the authority to give eternal life to all who follow him. Father and Son may have had different roles during his 30+ years on Earth but, in substance, they were eternally inseparable and one God.

Jesus clearly knew the Father in a deep, intimate way. It therefore would not have been difficult for him to exercise complete trust in his Father in any and every situation that presented itself. And it is no wonder that Jesus lay peacefully asleep during a violent squall, even if he was aware of the wind and waves. He had absolute confidence that his Father's love and power would protect him.

## TRUST IN THE TRINITY

This leads us to an important question: is that level of peace and confidence in God's love and protection available to us as well? Can we know the Father in the same way that Jesus did? Can we know the Godhead with the same love and trust as they enjoy with one another?

The last words of Jesus to his disciples in terms of an extended teaching time can be found on the night he was arrested. During the Last Supper

---

[65] John 5:17

[66] John 10:30

[67] "For this reason, they tried all the more to kill him; not only was he breaking the Sabbath, but he was even calling God his own Father, making himself equal with God" (John 5:18).

[68] John 5:22

and along the streets after. Starting in John 14, we eavesdrop on Jesus' final opportunity to impart some truths before he is taken from them.

The discourse starts with Jesus telling his disciples that he is preparing a place where they will dwell both with him and with the Father. He suggests that they know how to get there. Thomas asks for clarification: "Lord, we don't know where you are going, so how can we know the way?"[69], to which Jesus responds with his famous words, "I am the way and the truth and the life. No one comes to the Father except through me."[70]

They can know the Father through Jesus. But Phillip presses Jesus further: "Lord, show us the Father and that will be enough for us."[71]And this question lays the foundation for the rest of the teaching conversation.

What strikes me is what Jesus doesn't say. He doesn't say, 'Here are seven ways you can know the Father like I do'. Essentially, he says, 'Everything you need to know about the Father, you can see in me'. In his words, "Anyone who has seen me has seen the Father."[72]

He then tells them that he is sending help. One who will live with them – the Spirit of truth.[73] Jesus is in the Father, he is in the disciples, and they are in him. The Spirit or 'comforter' will dwell among them and *in* them. Even though the Father's house has many rooms (a reference to the life to come), Jesus told his friends that the Father will love them "and we will come to them and make our home with them" (a reference to their life and ministry on Earth).[74]

The disciples and subsequent believers in Christ are invited into relationship with Christ and therefore also with the Father and the Spirit. And

---

[69] John 14:5
[70] John 14:6
[71] John 14:8
[72] John 14:9
[73] John 14:17
[74] John 14:23

for any troubles that might occur during their time on the planet, we are told, "Peace I leave with you; my peace I give you. I do not give to you as the world gives. Do not let your hearts be troubled and do not be afraid."[75]

I wonder if Jesus was hoping the events on the boat would come to mind as he said those words. 'Don't be afraid. Don't let your hearts be troubled. Disciples – I had peace that day because I knew the Father's loving presence with me. You can experience my peace too. It is not a human thing. It is not a peace that the world gives. It comes from me. I freely give it to you. Just don't *let* your hearts be troubled.'

## A GIFT FROM THE GODHEAD

A year after her diagnosis, Janet shared something of her journey with a group of friends. She told them that, on her way to the doctor to hear the news she had suspected, she prayed a prayer: 'Lord, I don't know what the future holds. I don't know if I've got months or decades to live but I do know I can trust you in everything that happens, so I'm surrendering this situation completely into your hands. You made this body. You know it and you know how many days you have written for me in your book. So, take this situation, Lord. Use it for your glory and give me your peace, and in return, I will trust you with whatever the future holds.'[76]

The treatment was full-on, with operations, spells in hospital, chemo and side effects, but Janet's testimony throughout was that she and her husband, Ian, experienced peace. One friend asked her if she was angry with God for the ordeal she was going through. She simply replied that she was grateful to God for his goodness. And she meant it. Another commented

---

[75] John 14:27
[76] Reproduced with permission

that she must be very brave. 'No,' she said, 'I'm not brave at all, but I am held, and I know who is holding me'.

Janet was keen to convey to her friends that the peace she experienced had nothing to do with any courage she might muster. It wasn't a super-spiritual thing. It was a supernatural thing, a gift from the Father, Son and Holy Spirit who promised her an eternal home. A peace that the world cannot give.

## PEACE THROUGH RELATIONSHIP

After Jesus had spoken about peace at the Last Supper, they all got up and left the house. The conversation continued. Walking along the road, Jesus started to describe to his disciples a relationship between himself, them and the Father, likening it to a vine producing grapes.

Jesus is the vine, and his followers are branches on that vine. The Father, an expert gardener, tends to it. He is at liberty to prune and cut as he sees fit so that together we can bear fruitful lives in the Kingdom of God. Jesus loves us with the same love he has with the Father. The Spirit sent from the Father will speak truth to us and glorify the Son. The picture is complete when we also commit to loving one another.

Jesus finished his discourse by assuring the disciples of the Father's love for them and with these final words: "I have told you these things, so that in me you may have peace. In this world you will have trouble. But take heart! I have overcome the world."[77]

'I have told you these things so that in me you may have peace.'

I have found myself thinking a lot about this. Why do some people experience miraculous peace against all logic, while others struggle to find

---

[77] John 16:33

it? Why do some followers of Jesus seem to bounce from one anxious state to another, while others find a place of quiet trust in God? I don't believe God has favourites but I do believe we can miss the gifts he wants to give us.

We can never earn it, but obedience and surrender to the Lord seems to be a factor. Jonah needed to repent of his disobedience to the Lord's command. Jesus constantly challenged his disciples to look past their doubt and fear. When we surrender our plans and wills to the purposes of God, maybe we can begin to rest in his sovereignty over life's events. Over the storms.

Jesus and his disciples continued their slow amble down the street, walking off their full stomachs from their meal. While describing the new relationship between himself, the Father and them, Jesus gave this command: "Remain in me, as I also remain in you."[78] He also exhorted his friends – and therefore us – with the words, "Ask whatever you wish, and it will be done for you."[79]

There seems to be an expectation here that the disciples will stay close to Jesus, despite his imminent departure. And keep asking for help. Perhaps the challenge for us today is whether we will actively and purposefully stay close to Jesus in our comings and goings of life. And will we continuously ask for help and guidance? Maybe it is in that intimacy that Paul discovered the secret of communion with God "in every situation, by prayer and petition, with thanksgiving," leading to his own supernatural peace.[80]

Remain in him. Not just a passing nod on a Sunday or an occasional prayer request, but a daily, walking relationship with the God who knows everything about you and would love you to know and experience much more about him.

---

[78]  John 15:4
[79]  John 15:7
[80]  Philippians 4:6

## Summary

- There was a deep love relationship shared by God the Father and God the Son.
- Jesus often spoke about the Father, even stating he was at one with him.
- Jesus would have had every confidence in his Father to guide and protect him.
- Jesus invites us into an ongoing relationship with the Father and the Spirit through faith in him, and in that relationship, he promises peace.

## Key Takeaway

When the storms of life strike, lean into the relationship you have been brought into.

# CHAPTER 6

# *Don't you care if we drown?*

The disciples woke him and said to him, "Teacher, don't you care if we drown?"

He got up, rebuked the wind and said to the waves, "Quiet! Be still!" Then the wind died down and it was completely calm.

He said to his disciples, "Why are you so afraid? Do you still have no faith?"[81]

It's a fair question by the disciples. 'Lord, have you noticed what's going on? We're going under, and you don't seem to be particularly concerned about it.'

After Jesus had stood and commanded the storm to abate, he gave his response. He could have said, 'Yes, of course I care about you. I don't want you to drown. There you go, all sorted!' Or perhaps he might have turned it into teaching opportunity: 'And that's how we deal with those pesky storms. Use the authority I have already given you.'

Instead, his reply sounded more like a rebuke: "Why are you so afraid? Do you still have no faith?"

---

[81] Mark 4:38–40

I wonder how Jesus pictured his disciples reacting to the situation in the ideal world. Did he honestly expect them to have no fear? Did he imagine calm spirits, despite the violent lurches of the hull driven by the pounding waves and the painful spray spitting in their eyes?

And bringing this story up to date for followers of Jesus today, does Jesus imagine that we will have hearts at peace during our storms, confident in the Fathers love and care in the same way that he experienced it that day on the lake?

Why are you so afraid, disciples? Where is your faith? Jesus did seem to be genuinely disappointed in his disciples' handling of the situation. Instead of quiet trust in the one sharing the boat with them, they woke him with an accusation and a panic-stricken cry, 'Lord, don't you care if we drown?' Instead of faith, they came to him in anger and fear.

But perhaps Jesus had a point. Even before he had begun to teach them about faith and about barriers to faith, they would have known the stories and wisdom literature from their Hebrew Scriptures (our Old Testament).

Let's look at two examples. For the first, we dive into the middle of a story about Israel's second king, David – actually, before he became king.

## FINDING STRENGTH IN GOD

Towards the end of the book of 1 Samuel, we find David and his army returning home to their families after an unsuccessful attempt to offer assistance to a friend about to go into battle. They lived in a place called Ziklag.

Ziklag was Philistine – enemy territory, where David and his men had been hiding from a jealous King Saul, who had been trying to kill him. It had been a questionable decision to live there because, as some have suggested, it revealed a lack of trust in God to protect him. But right or wrong, that's what David had decided to do.

As they approached Ziklag, they realised the unthinkable had happened. While they had been away, the Amalekites had paid them am unfriendly visit and "they found it destroyed by fire and their wives and sons and daughters taken captive. So, David and his men wept aloud until they had no strength left to weep."[82]

And if that wasn't bad enough, we are then told "David was greatly distressed because the men were talking of stoning him; each one was bitter in spirit because of his sons and daughters."[83]

This is extreme pressure. Even men loyal to David began to turn on him.

But David's response is quite remarkable: 'David found strength in the Lord his God'.[84]

Imagine the stress David would have been under. The fear of harm coming to his loved ones. The guilt of feeling that it was all his fault ('if only I had trusted God and stayed away from Philistine territory') and the pain of close friends turning on him.

But David found strength in the Lord his God. How did he do that?

The text doesn't answer that question, so we don't know for sure, but we do know the sort of things David prayed when he was in trouble in the form of his psalms. In this terrible and intense situation, I imagine David finding peace and wisdom in God (and therefore strength to move forward) with words of prayer similar to those we find in Psalm 25, particularly the first seven verses.

> In you, LORD my God,
> I put my trust.
> I trust in you;

---

[82]   1 Samuel 30:3–4
[83]   Verse 6a
[84]   Verse 6b

do not let me be put to shame,
nor let my enemies triumph over me.
No one who hopes in you
will ever be put to shame,
but shame will come on those
who are treacherous without cause.
Show me your ways, LORD,
teach me your paths.
Guide me in your truth and teach me,
for you are God my Saviour,
and my hope is in you all day long.
Remember, LORD, your great mercy and love,
for they are from of old.
Do not remember the sins of my youth
and my rebellious ways;
according to your love remember me,
for you, LORD, are good.

The psalm begins with, "In you, Lord my God, I put my trust." If this was David's prayer in 1 Samuel 30, his first thought is not to stare at the problem but to declare the sovereignty of God. He is Lord. 'You are the Lord and you are my God.'

He then expresses his trust in God, both in the first verse and at the beginning of the next. It is a determined declaration: 'I trust you. I speak out with my mouth what I believe in my heart.' He expresses trust in the God who saves, heals and delivers.

Next, David pleads, 'Do not let me be put to shame, nor let my enemies triumph over me'. Davd knows he is not just facing a battle against a physical enemy but also against the inner battles of fear, guilt, and doubt. 'Lord, I am sharing my heart with you. Don't let these enemies win.'

Then he asks, 'Show me your ways, Lord, teach me your paths. Guide me in your truth and teach me, for you are God my Savior, and my hope is in you all day long.' In other words, 'Lord, show me what to do. I don't want to be driven by passion or revenge; I want to know your perfect plan in this situation.'

In the next verse he asks, 'Remember, Lord, your great mercy and love, for they are from of old'. Here David is expressing faith in God's character. God doesn't need to be reminded of who he is, but David appeals to the truths he knows about God. Having declared the sovereignty of God, David now speaks to him of his character.

God is a God of mercy. God is a God of love. That has always been the case and it always will be. In this terrifying moment David knows he can put his trust in those truths.

Finally, in this part of Psalm 25, he prays, 'Do not remember the sins of my youth and my rebellious ways; according to your love remember me, for you, Lord, are good.'

David's faith is not in his own righteousness, he knows he deserves nothing. His faith is in the love of God and the goodness of God.

In summary, David declared the truth of who God is and expressed his faith in him. He then confidently asked for his help whilst reminding himself of the Lord's love and goodness. Perhaps that is how he found strength in the Lord his God: he declared truth first, faith second, then asked him for the guidance and help he needed whilst continuing to remind himself of God's love and goodness.

## TRUSTING HIM WITH ALL OF YOUR HEART

With such an example in their nation's history, perhaps Jesus hoped his disciples might be those who would subconsciously model their lives on the great heroes of old like David. When a metaphorical storm hit David, he found strength in God. Why couldn't the disciples find the same strength and trust in Jesus or the Father?

Some might argue that meditating on a story like that is still not enough as we face the storms of life. We can declare truths, speak them out loud, remind ourselves of God's sovereignty and affirm our trust in him. But what if our hearts still want to submit to the fear and doubt? Like the disciples.

I wonder how familiar the disciples were with these verses in Proverbs 3:

> Trust in the LORD with all your heart
> and lean not on your own understanding;
> in all your ways submit to him,
> and he will make your paths straight.[85]

Christians are not immune to finding it hard to trust God in the situations that they face. It is not that God is untrustworthy, but rather that we can sometimes struggle to look away from the things that make us anxious, and instead rest in the peace God wants to give us.

But perhaps these two verses can be helpful to us. In just a few words, they give us three instructions that help us obey Jesus' teaching in The Sermon on the Mount when he said, "Do not worry about your life ..."[86]

The first instruction is to "trust in the Lord *with all your heart*". As we have suggested, we can speak out our faith in God in difficult circumstances

---

[85] Proverbs 3:5–6
[86] Matthew 6:25

and we can read stories of others who have remained steadfast, hanging on to the promises of the Lord through life's challenges. But sometimes the concept of trust goes no further than in our heads. We might know we need to express faith in God, so we meditate on relevant verses of Scripture and say them or pray them out loud. But it doesn't reach our emotions. God wants us to trust him from the depths of our heart. How do we do that?

One way that I find helpful is to think about those attributes of God's character that particularly speak to the human heart. Here are a couple that speak to me.

First, God is kind. Following the Lords severe judgment of the nation of Israel by way of their Babylonian captivity, he made this promise to his children through the prophet Isaiah:

> "In a surge of anger
> I hid my face from you for a moment,
> but with everlasting kindness
> I will have compassion on you,"
> says the LORD your Redeemer.[87]

This is a powerful reminder that God is a God of compassion, and that his everlasting kindness is always directed towards his people – always directed towards us. Therefore, he will treat you and me kindly in our situation. Sometimes I just need to stop and remind myself that God is kind. He is a God of compassion. He will be kind and compassionate towards me because that is his nature.

Second, God is faithful. What does it mean that God is faithful? Deuteronomy 7:9 reminds us that '...he is the faithful God, keeping his

---

[87]   Isaiah 54:8

covenant of love to a thousand generations of those who love him and keep his commandments.'

A thousand generations is a very long time. If five generations is about a hundred years, then a thousand must be at least two hundred times that. That's 20,000 years! As Christians, our spiritual roots come from God's chosen people in the Scriptures, way back to the beginning of history, and then from Christ himself. If our spiritual roots are in Jesus, it is worth remembering that he perfectly loved his Father and kept his commandments. Therefore, God faithfully keeps his covenant of love with him and therefore, also with us.

God is faithful to us because he is faithful to his Son and to his people. Therefore, God will be faithful to us, in each of our situations. He will not let us down. He sees it all and knows how to work it out.

That being true, I can trust him with all my heart. And the promise is that he will make our paths straight. We don't need to be zigzagging all over the place, trying to find peace or struggling to make a decision. Just as David found strength in God, and, in the peace that followed, was able to work out the next decision he needed to make. Just as Jesus trusted his Father with all his heart and was quickly able to see his next course of action – calming the storm by word of command.

## MY LIMITED UNDERSTANDING

The second instruction in this short proverb is to 'lean not on your own understanding'. In other words, I need to look beyond the limits of my thinking and imagination. I have found that simple trust in God during challenging circumstances can be easily killed by allowing my mind to wander. When I think I understand every part of the situation. When I cannot see a way through. When I make assumptions about other people (usually incorrect ones). When I put too much confidence in my own understanding of what is going on.

A friend of mine tells the story of working with a person whose attitude towards him seemed uncaring, rude and even at times hostile. He wondered what he had done to offend him and even became afraid of saying the wrong thing. He felt he had to walk on eggshells around him and struggled to come to terms with the thought that a Christian brother would behave like this workmate.

However, one day he realised his partner was displaying some symptoms of a common mental health condition. A well-known neurological disorder. The man wasn't meaning to be rude – his brain was just wired differently. With a little more understanding of the situation, my friend was able to pray for a new perspective and trust God for a way forward.

When we focus only on what we *think* we know, when we forget to question our assumptions, when we believe we have all the facts (when often we don't), it is easy to lean on our own understanding, instead of trusting God to solve the puzzle from the view he has of the bigger picture.

Seeking the Lord for his understanding is so much better than making judgments with only a handful of the facts.

The third line of this proverb simply tells us to submit to him. In all our ways. This sounds to me like a reminder that he is Lord. Lord of me. The Scriptures constantly tell us that the Lord is on his throne and that Jesus reigns at the right hand of the Father. He is sovereign, no-one is higher than him. But sometimes we need to consciously submit our lives, our decisions, all of our problems and all of our comings and goings to his Lordship.

Regardless of how we may want a situation to play out, the Lord wants us to come to a place where we can say, 'Your will be done, on earth as it is in heaven.[88] 'You are a kind and good God, and you have your perfect

---

[88] Matthew 6:10

will. You have greater knowledge than I will ever have. While I sometimes base decisions on my assumptions, you see the actual truth. So, I submit my ways to you.'

## HANDING OVER THE PACKAGE

I had been planning the meeting for some time. I had made my preparations, thought about it and prayed about it, but I couldn't stop playing conversations over and over in my mind. These weren't real conversations, of course. They were the ones I hoped might not happen. If I said this, and he replied with that, then we go down that path and nothing good will come of it.

I told myself to stop inventing scenarios that were imaginary. That strategy worked for a couple of minutes until a new unpleasant thought entered the arena. On and on it went. I knew Jesus didn't want me to worry, but my worrying was on steroids.

My wife and I jumped in the car to get some food and while we were driving to the shops, she knew I had something on my mind. I told her everything, every one of my concerns. I poured it all out. In her gracious way, she reminded me that I have a propensity towards doing this and she helped me to realise that I wasn't really trusting in God to be Lord of the meeting and for his will to be carried out.

I had been making assumptions and worrying about possibilities. I had not left it all in his loving care. I had forgotten that he is kind and compassionate and faithful.

So, in my mind's eye, I handed something to him. I don't recall what it was now, perhaps a package. In that package were all my concerns, but also my trust in his goodness and ability to carry out his will.

The meeting was not due to start until later that evening but, during the next couple of hours, I experienced a peace I had not felt for a while.

Jesus does care if we drown, just as he cared about his friends and disciples on the day of the storm. But he is looking for faith – and sometimes the storms come because he wants our faith to grow.

## Summary

- The disciples would likely have been familiar with Old Testament stories of faith. Maybe Jesus expected them to draw inspiration from them during the life-threatening situation of the storm.
- David learned to trust God by expressing truth and faith, then asking for the guidance and help he needed, whilst continuing to remind himself of God's love and goodness.
- The Book of Proverbs encourages us to trust in the Lord with all our heart. We can do that by meditating on the attributes of God that speak directly to the human heart like his kindness and faithfulness.
- When we think about the Lord's compassion and goodness, we can give our worries to him.

## Key takeaway

When the storms of life strike, remember how God has been faithful to those who came before you.

# CHAPTER 7

# Quiet! Be Still!

## NOW *THAT'S* AUTHORITY!

My first career was serving as a high school science teacher in Southern England, and I remember vividly the first time I stood in a classroom laboratory filled with 30 spotty 13-year-olds, seated and (sort of) ready for their next lesson.

I was not confident. In fact, I didn't even look at the children, more the end of the bench I was standing behind as I mumbled some instructions trying to get them to settle down. 'OK, listen now! Errmm, can you listen, please? Shhhh!'

No effect.

I kept going, raising my voice in degrees as I attempted to make myself heard among the loud chatter in the room, until suddenly the noise died down. There was a hush.

'This is it', I thought, 'Success! They're listening to me now. I can do this.'

Until I noticed that no-one was looking at me. Every student had his eyes fixed on the door to my left. As I glanced over, I was met with the vision of the principal (we called them headmasters in the UK), standing fully robed in an old-fashioned schoolmaster's batman-type black cape and staring at me.

I can't remember what happened next. Probably some announcement was given to the class before Batman wafted away down the corridor, but I do remember thinking, 'Now *that* is authority!'

When people compared Jesus to the religious leaders of the day, they noticed something important. He had authority. In Chapter One, we noted his ability to cast out evil spirits and heal the sick. He also had no qualms pronouncing the forgiveness of sins.

Mark is particularly good at noticing this in his gospel. While Jesus was teaching in the synagogue in Capernaum, we are told that 'the people were amazed at his teaching, because he taught them as one who had authority, not as the teachers of the law'.[89] When a man with an impure spirit cried out, Jesus commanded the spirit to be quiet. After it came out of him, the people marvelled even more: "What is this? A new teaching—and with authority! He even gives orders to impure spirits, and they obey him."[90]

Mark also describes the moment when Jesus was teaching in a house packed with people, and a paralysed man was lowered through a hole in the roof by friends who hoped that he might heal him. Jesus did the miracle, but not before pronouncing the forgiveness of sins over the man, something only God has the authority to do. Knowing the teachers of the Law were struggling with this, he calmly asked, "Which is easier: to say to this paralysed man, Your sins are forgiven," 'or to say, 'Get up, take your mat and walk'? But I want you to know that the Son of Man has authority on earth to forgive sins." So, he said to the man, "I tell you, get up, take your

---

[89]  Mark 1:22
[90]  Mark 1:27

mat and go home." He got up, took his mat and walked out in full view of them all.[91]

Fast forward to the day on the lake and the nasty storm and, although the command to the evil spirit is a different word in the original Greek, Jesus also commanded the wind and waves to be quiet. Because he had the authority to do so.

How does this help us? Simply this: Jesus called his disciples to follow him.[92] In some contexts, we might use these words to describe passively watching somebody, perhaps in the same way a person 'follows' a football team. But in Jesus' eyes, it meant practical action. Jesus wanted his followers to learn to do what he was doing. He wasn't just trying to fill their heads with knowledge or new ideas; he was training them for action.

We can see that, as Mark again communicates it to us: "Jesus went up on a mountainside and called to him those he wanted, and they came to him. He appointed twelve that they might be with him and that he might send them out to preach and to have authority to drive out demons."[93]

The 'sending out' occurred a few chapters later: "They went out and preached that people should repent. They drove out many demons and anointed many sick people with oil and healed them."[94]

Notice that Jesus didn't just train his followers to try and emulate him, although that is partly what he was doing. Mark tells us that he gave them authority. He gave his disciples the authority that he had to preach, heal the sick and drive out demons.

---

[91]  Mark 2:8–12
[92]  For example, in Mark 1:17
[93]  Mark 3:13–16
[94]  Mark 6:12–13

## USING THE AUTHORITY THAT JESUS HAD

The way Jesus used his authority was interesting, particularly in healing the sick. He healed Simon Peter's mother-in-law, sick in bed with a fever, by taking her hand and helping her get up. To the man with leprosy, he simply said, 'Be clean!' To the leper lowered in from the roof of the house, he gave the command to pick up the mat he had been lying on and go home.

He told the man with the shrivelled hand to stretch it out, he took the seriously ill little girl by the hand and instructed her to get up, and after putting spit on a deaf and mute man's tongue, he commanded his ears to be opened.

Much has been made of the methods Jesus used to perform healing miracles, but perhaps what is worth noting is that, when the age of the church began after Jesus had died on the cross, was raised from the dead and ascended into heaven, the disciples really did emulate him. They didn't pray, 'Lord Jesus, please heal this person'. They took action and spoke words that commanded the healing.

For example, to the lame man at the temple gate, Peter said, "In the name of Jesus Christ of Nazareth, walk."[95] To Aeneas, the man bedridden for eight years, Peter said, "Jesus Christ heals you. Get up and roll up your mat."[96] The book of Acts records other miracles occurring at the command of Philip and Paul. At one time, Paul threw himself onto a young man who had suffered a fatal fall and the man was restored.

Jesus gave the authority he had to his disciples and, as we see in Acts, those who also will come to believe, to do the things he did. Does that mean we have the same authority as Jesus to still wind and waves in a dan-

---

[95] Acts 3:6
[96] Acts 9:34

gerous storm? To fight supernaturally against elements that create storms in our lives?

I think it does. In the second chapter of Ephesians, after some devastating verses about our spiritual condition before faith in Christ, when people can only be described as 'the living dead', we are told that God made us alive. Spiritually speaking, he put the defibrillator paddles on us and restored us to life. But there's more: "And God raised us up with Christ and seated us with him in the heavenly realms in Christ Jesus, in order that in the coming ages he might show the incomparable riches of his grace, expressed in his kindness to us in Christ Jesus."[97]

When we put our faith in Jesus Christ for the forgiveness of our sins, confessing our belief that he took the punishment for them before rising from the dead, the Lord not only forgave us and removed our sins from us, he also broke the power of sin and restored our relationship with him, even seating us 'in Christ' where he is reigning at the right hand of the Father. Where he is in charge. Where he has all authority.

Spiritually speaking, we have the authority Christ gave to his disciples to do the things he did during his three plus years on ministry on earth, and probably a lot more. Why? Because we are raised up with him to the place of all authority.

I think another reason Jesus could sleep peacefully in the boat, while the elements sought to tear it apart is because he knew that a command from him was all it would take to change everything. I wonder if we can have the same confidence in our storms.

Perhaps it comes down to two things: a sensitivity to the Father's will in a situation through the leading of the Holy Spirit, and then the faith that our spoken word can result in a miraculous change. A healing. A mountain being moved. Or a storm fading to nothing.

---

[97] Ephesians 2:6-7

At a time when mines were closing in Western Australia in the late 1990s, many people were laid off work and Sam was one of them. New jobs were in short supply and Sam found himself unemployed. There was just enough money coming into the household, but Sam and his family were living hand-to-mouth.

Six months later and, with still no hope of a job on the horizon, Sam started experiencing some strange dreams. Disturbing dreams. And they were always the same one.

In the dream, Sam was in the house where he grew up in his village in Ghana. His mother was there with the rest of his family, including his late brother who had died nearly 20 years before. The brother was always in the dream but never spoke to anyone because he was also dead in the dream. In this surreal scene, Sam realised he was living with a dead person. 'That's ok,' he thought, 'it's only a dream.' Except it wasn't! There was something about it that felt very real to Sam every time he woke up.

The vivid dream kept repeating, over and over, and it became a little frightening. Eventually Sam addressed his dead brother in the dream. 'You shouldn't be here. Why are you here?' but there was no answer. Initially, the dream occurred two or three times each week but soon increased to four or five times per week.

As the frequency of the dreams increased, there was no progress in finding the work Sam desperately needed. Although this father of four had the qualifications and the experience, job application after job application was turned down. No doors were opening. Time continued to pass.

On one particular morning, Sam opened his Bible and began reading. He worshipped for a while but was then overcome with a strong compulsion to go back to sleep. With heavy eyelids, he walked back to his bedroom and fell onto his bed. Then the strangest thing happened.

As he lay there, he experienced a sensation that felt like two hands applying pressure to his head. Sam felt he was being pushed into his pillow. At this point, he could sense the presence of the Lord. He spoke out loud, but felt it was the Holy Spirit speaking through him: 'I rebuke you in the name of Jesus!'

Immediately, the sense of pressure disappeared, and Sam was startled by the sharp movement of something in the room. As he turned his head toward it (a 'foul spirit', he called it), he saw a sort of grey, distorted human-like form without any well-defined features that lingered a while before sinking and disappearing into the earth. Whether this was another dream Sam was experiencing or an awareness of the spiritual realm, Sam doesn't know. But he does know that finally he felt calm, and his fear vanished.

Three days later, he received a call, asking him to attend an interview and, three weeks later, he had a job. After 18 months unemployment.

The dreams never returned.

## AUTHORITY AND THE HOLY SPIRIT

What do you do with a story like that? As Sam and I enjoyed a cup of tea in the warm, spring sunshine in his back garden, he was keen to tell me that the Holy Spirit was the one who set him free from his storm. The evil presence that had haunted his dreams and somehow managed to prevent him from stepping through doors of employment, was quickly dispelled as he spoke under the power and anointing of God's Spirit. Sam rebuked the evil presence with the authority that the Lord gave him, and it had no choice but to flee. Sam's peace returned and his circumstances began to change,

We agreed, on reflection, that speaking with the Lord's authority must be a Holy Spirit inspired moment. In Acts 4, Peter, 'filled with the Holy

Spirit', managed to declare the truth of Jesus and answer questions about the crippled man being healed.[98] Luke tells us that Barnabas and Paul were sent out on their first missionary journey after the Holy Spirit said, "Set apart for me Barnabas and Saul for the work to which I have called them."[99]

Like the first disciples, Jesus gives us his authority to speak and command change but it must be under the anointing and leading of the Holy Spirit.

Can we speak to a storm or a hurricane bearing down upon us and command it to stop? Perhaps we can, if that is what the Spirit is telling us to do. If that is the Lord's will in that situation. One thing is for sure: we as Christians probably have more authority to declare change as the Lord leads than most of us realise. I suspect we *under*use the authority and power that is available to us to do his kingdom work.

Perhaps one reason Jesus allowed his disciples to experience his command of the storm was to show them in powerful reality what a life in close relationship with the Godhead looks like. Remember, Jesus would eventually say to them on the last night before he was arrested: "Truly, truly, I say to you, whoever believes in me will also do the works that I do; and greater works than these will he do, because I am going to the Father. Whatever you ask in my name, this I will do, that the Father may be glorified in the Son. If you ask me anything in my name, I will do it."[100]

## Summary

- Jesus could calm the storm by a word of command because he had the authority to do so, in the same way that he could command a healing to take place.

---

[98] Acts 4:8
[99] Acts 13:2,
[100] John 14:12–14

- Jesus gave the same authority to his disciples. We see them using that authority to do miracles in the book of Acts.
- Through faith in Christ's death on the cross and resurrection, we are now spiritually placed 'in Christ' in the heavenly realms, next to the Father. We have all the spiritual authority that comes with that.
- Jesus said that those who believe in him will do the works he did.

## Key Takeaway

When the storms of life strike, be open to the leading of the Holy Spirit and remember the authority you have in Christ to declare change.

# CHAPTER 8
## *Who is this?*

## GOD OUR REFUGE

Throughout the Old Testament, in numerous examples, the Lord is a protector. The Bible contains several Hebrew words that can be translated into English as 'a strong, safe place', each with slightly different nuances.

*Misgab* conveys the idea of an elevated platform, tall enough to keep people out of reach from enemies in battle. It is sometimes translated as 'a high tower, a defence, a stronghold or fortress'.

*Manos* is a place of escape, somewhere to flee towards.

The verb, *chasah*, conveys the idea of a person putting their trust in something or someone, especially the Lord.

Each of these words can be translated as 'refuge'. David used all three in his song of celebration, thanking the Lord for his deliverance from the Philistines and from the hands of a jealous King Saul in 1 Samuel 22:2b–3:

> The LORD is my rock, my fortress and my deliverer;
> my God is my rock, in whom I take refuge,
> my shield and the horn of my salvation.

He is my stronghold, my refuge and my saviour—
from violent people you save me.

The Lord is our refuge too – a place of safety like a high impenetrable tower, a place to escape to as one fleeing from danger, a place where we can trust that no harm will come to us. As the prophet Nahum declared: "The LORD is good, a refuge in times of trouble. He cares for those who trust in him."[101]

The concept of God as a refuge also includes the description of him as a shelter or protection from fierce rain and storm.

You have been a refuge for the poor,
a refuge for the needy in their distress,
a shelter from the storm
and a shade from the heat.[102]

The Lord is a safe shelter for all those facing the calamities or afflictions of life, likened here to a tempest of wind and rain.

Psalm 46 describes catastrophic events that can be evocative of natural disasters like landslides, tsunamis or earthquakes. The earth gives away, the mountains quake and waters roar and foam. But the Lord is more powerful than any of them.

'Come and see what the LORD has done,' calls the psalmist, 'the desolations he has brought on the earth,' describing his ability to bring wars to an end.[103] However, the point of the psalm is not primarily to exalt God's greatness and power (which it does very well) but to encourage his people that he is the one they can turn to, whatever the circumstances around them.

---

[101] Nahum 1:7
[102] Isaiah 25:4
[103] Psalm 46:8

God is our refuge and strength, an ever-present help in trouble. Therefore, we will not fear, though the earth give way, and the mountains fall into the heart of the sea, though its waters roar and foam and the mountains quake with their surging.[104]

Landslides and earthquakes can move the ground beneath our feet, the oceans can lift their waves and threaten the sturdiest of ships, but God is our refuge. He is present, ever-present, stronger than any natural phenomenon.

The psalm concludes with the climactic call and declaration

Be still and know that I am God;
I will be exalted among the nations,
I will be exalted in the earth.[105]

Be still! Where have we heard that before?

## THE PRESENCE OF THE LORD

When Jesus displayed no fear of the storm and commanded the wind and waves to stop, it cannot have passed unnoticed that only God has no fear of mountains falling and especially waters roaring and foaming. The Lord not only provides shelter from the storm, but he can exercise his authority over it. The moment Jesus spoke to the storm, he betrayed his identity.

That day on a lake in Galilee, reeling unsteadily as their boat was buffeted by powerful waves, the disciples had not yet realised who was in the boat with them: The Lord, their refuge and strength was there. So Jesus takes it to the next level by commanding the storm to be still. In effect, he

---

[104] Psalm 46:1–3
[105] Psalms 46:10

is saying, 'I am not only your refuge, but I can also control the elements that threaten your life. Be still and know that I am God. Storm – be still! Disciples – know that I am God.'

The Lord showed himself to be present in an entirely new and unique way. No wonder the terrified disciples asked "Who is this? Even the wind and waves obey him."

The God of their ancestors was present in front of them, and they didn't know it.

The Bible has some interesting things to say about the presence of the Lord, times when the Lord manifested himself in a tangible way. God's presence was seen in a fire and cloud that accompanied the Israelites in the wilderness and the glory of the Lord also filled the tabernacle and the temple.

Sometimes his presence was experienced through particular supernatural events where the laws of nature were changed. In a psalm often sung before Passover meals, the author of Psalm 114 reminds us of the Israelites' rescue from Egypt and God's miraculous provision during the wilderness years and entry into the Promised Land.

Under Moses' leadership, we are told that the Re(e)d Sea 'looked and fled'[106], and under Joshua's command, the priests carrying the ark of the Covenant came to the water's edge and the "water from upstream stopped flowing. It piled up a great distance away."[107] These are clearly miraculous events, beyond the natural course of things.

The psalmist, curiously addressing both the Red Sea and the River Jordan, asks an intriguing question: "Why was it, sea that you fled? Why Jordan did you turn back?".[108] It is as if the poet is transporting himself

---

[106] Verse 3a
[107] Joshua 3:16
[108] Psalm 114:5

back in time, imagining each moment, marvelling at the spectacle and asking, 'How did this happen?'. Even asking the water for an explanation. 'Why, sea/river did you do it? Why break every instinct of nature?'

The psalmist is not slow to provide his own answer: "Tremble, earth, at the presence of the Lord, at the presence of the God of Jacob."[109] God was there. God was present. No other explanation is offered or necessary. God's supernatural presence appeared in such a profound way that water and gravity abandoned their own physical laws and obeyed a new command from the Lord.

What conclusion can we draw? Simply this: the universe obeys mathematical and scientific laws because that's how God created it, but those laws can be superseded in a moment by his presence. If we are not careful, we can put more faith in the rules of nature (which God created) than in the mind-blowing and infinite possibilities that lie in his all-powerful presence.

This can surely help us in our prayers. To know that God's presence can overshadow any natural law. To know that his will and his power can take the throne in a situation over even the created order of the universe. When we pray, God transports us to a world of new, varied and infinite possibilities.

## CHANGING THE LAWS OF NATURE

As the elements of wind and water swirled around a small, fragile fishing vessel containing twelve disciples and the Son of God, Jesus simply addressed the wind and waves, "Quiet! Be still!" All atoms set in their courses were compelled to follow a higher power in that moment. Then the wind died down and it was completely calm."[110]

---

[109] Psalm 114:7
[110] Mark 4:39

I like the fact that there is order in the world around me; that the sun will rise tomorrow and that the bruise on my shoulder will likely heal without any help from me. I can time the eggs boiling on my stove because one second and one minute are not going to change their lengths. Nature's predictability gives me permission to make plans.

But thank God that his intervening presence is also possible, like when water and air molecules, synchronizing as a furious storm, decide to break their natural laws of motion simply because a word had been uttered by a higher power. Thank the Lord that miracles are not bedtime stories, that situations can change when God shows up in a supernatural way.

The disciples were left more perplexed after their boat journey than before as to who their master really was, but we in the 21ˢᵗ century, have the advantages of a full canon of Scripture and millennia of theological reflection.

In time, Paul would describe Jesus as the 'image of the invisible God'.[111] John, reflecting on the identity of Christ in his gospel wrote, "No one has ever seen God. The one and only Son, who is himself God and is at the Father's side—he has revealed him."[112] 1600 hundred years later, the Westminster Assembly[113] would write, 'In the unity of the Godhead there be three persons of one substance, power, and eternity: God the Father, God the Son, and God the Holy Ghost'.[114]

Jesus has all the power and authority that the God of the Old Testament had when the Lord parted the Red Sea and filled the temple with his glory. Because they are of one substance. And he, through the presence of the

---

[111] Colossians 1:15
[112] John 1:18 (Christian Standard Bible)
[113] A council of English theologians and members of parliament appointed from 1643 to 1653 to restructure the Church of England.
[114] Westminster Confession of Faith chapter II, section III.

Holy Spirit, rides the storms with us, unafraid, never confused and always knowing his Father's purposes.

The Lord who created the universe and wields all the power to control it is with us in the mess of every squall we encounter. If we are not conscious of his presence, we can run to him and find shelter. We can take refuge in him when his sovereignty determines that the storm must rage for a while and, when the time is right, we can experience the miracles of atoms changing their courses.

## SOVEREIGN OVER ALL THINGS

Eric was late for an important meeting at the other end of the city. He pulled his car into busy traffic and looked at the clock on his dashboard. He guessed his likely average speed for the next thirty minutes or so and estimated the distance he needed to travel to get to his destination. Every calculation had him showing up late.

So he prayed and found peace as he decided to stop watching the clock. 'I will trust in God to get me there on time.'

When Eric shares his story, he still can't explain how he managed to arrive without being late. It is as if God did something strange with the flow of time. According to Eric, Jesus is not only sovereign over atoms and molecules and over the storms of life but also even sovereign over time itself.

We are not alone when the storms of life appear unannounced and uninvited. God our refuge can keep us safe and enable us to find a place of calm during the ordeal. God as sovereign can speak change into the natural laws that shape the situation. As the Holy Spirit leads and enables, we too can command change within the storms we face.

We have said it before: sometimes we just need to remember who is in the boat with us.

## Summary

- There are several references in the Old Testament to God being our refuge.
- Miracles can happen when the Lord is present.

## Key Takeaway

When the storms of life strike, the one who is with us is God, our refuge, who is sovereign over all things.

# CHAPTER 9

## *The Sign of Jonah*

### SHOW ME A SIGN

I like the (probably) fictional story of the man who was trapped in his house during a serious flood. The nearby river's banks had burst and the waters were rising, entering businesses and homes. Help was on its way for those who were stranded, but nobody knew how long they would have to wait.

The man retreated upstairs to the second floor and prayed God would give him a sign from heaven that he would be ok. Eventually, as flood waters continued to rise, the man climbed out of an upstairs window and managed to scramble on to the roof. 'Lord, I trust you for a miraculous sign that I am going to survive this. Please speak to me, Lord.'

About twenty minutes later, a couple of people in a boat stopped next to the house. 'Get in,' they shouted, but the man declined the offer. 'God is going to rescue me. I am just waiting for his sign.' 'OK,' they replied, rather perplexed and paddled away.

Then a helicopter arrived and hovered above the house. A rope ladder was lowered to the man. 'Thanks,' he shouted, 'but I'll be ok. I've asked

God for a sign that he will rescue me. I'm waiting for him to speak. My faith is in the Lord.'

The occupants of the helicopter couldn't persuade the man to climb the ladder, so they reluctantly continued on to offer assistance to other stranded residents.

Eventually, the floodwaters rose so high that the man realised his house would soon be completely engulfed and underwater. Discouraged that the Lord had been silent, the man caught a ride on the next boat that passed that way.

Later that day, he had opportunity to reflect on his adventure and he asked the Lord in prayer why he had let him down. 'Lord, I asked for a sign that you would do a miracle and rescue me, but nothing happened. You didn't speak to me. There was no sign. There was no message from you.'

'I sent you a boat and a helicopter,' replied the Lord. 'What more do you want?'

A silly story perhaps, but the trouble with asking the Lord for a sign is that, more often than not, we have an idea in our minds as to what that sign *should* look like. How we think God should answer our request. A bit like the religious leaders' expectations of a Messiah in Jesus' day.

> Then some of the Pharisees and teachers of the law said to him (Jesus), "Teacher, we want to see a sign from you." He answered, "A wicked and adulterous generation asks for a sign! But none will be given it except the sign of the prophet Jonah. For as Jonah was three days and three nights in the belly of a huge fish, so the Son of Man will be three days and three nights in the heart of the earth. The men of Nineveh will stand up at the judgment with

this generation and condemn it; for they repented at the preaching of Jonah, and now something greater than Jonah is here".[115]

'A wicked and adulterous generation asks for a sign!' said Jesus. In the previous story of a crippled man lowered through a roof for Jesus to heal, when the Pharisees took objection to Jesus proclaiming forgiveness, we are told that Jesus 'knew in his spirit... what they were thinking in their hearts'.[116] If Jesus can discern a person's thinking, he could probably picture the type of sign the religious leaders had in their thoughts too. So, what did the Pharisees and teachers of the law imagine when they demanded Jesus give them a sign?

In short, the Pharisees wanted proof that Jesus was the Messiah. The type of Messiah they saw in the Old Testament. This Messiah might call down fire from heaven like in the story of Elijah[117] or part the Red Sea as in the days of Moses. He might overthrow Roman rule with the same heroism as a young David slew Goliath the Philistine.

But Jesus' answer could only have confused them. The one sign coming will relate to the ancient prophet, Jonah. The guy who disobeyed, effectively died, got swallowed by a fish and then reappeared, apparently having come back to life. The only sign they will receive is one of death and resurrection. The ministry of the Messiah will not be characterised by heroes wielding divine fire, halting mighty rivers or killing giants. It will reach its climax through humility and death.

---

[115] Matthew 12:38–41
[116] See Mark 2:8
[117] 1 Kings 18:38

That's what Isaiah had prophesied. The Messiah will be a hero – but not in the way the teachers of law imagined it. He will be despised and suffer, rejected and familiar with pain.[118]

Later the Pharisees came back again, asking him to show them 'a sign from heaven'.[119] Matthew tells us they were deliberately testing him.

> He replied, "When evening comes, you say, 'It will be fair weather, for the sky is red,' and in the morning, 'Today it will be stormy, for the sky is red and overcast.' You know how to interpret the appearance of the sky, but you cannot interpret the signs of the times. A wicked and adulterous generation looks for a sign, but none will be given it except the sign of Jonah." Jesus then left them and went away.[120]

'You can predict the weather,' says Jesus to the Pharisees, 'by simply looking at the sky at sunrise and sunset. But you can't read the signs of the times. Look around you. Look at the miracles, the teachings, the clues I have already given you. But I know you are struggling to read them so, there is one massive sign still to come. Something that will remind you of Jonah.'

I imagine Jesus, at that point, looking ahead and hoping and praying that revelation would eventually come to them following his death and resurrection. Perhaps it did for some.

---

[118] See Isaiah 53:3
[119] Matthew 16:1
[120] Matthew 16:2–4

## THE SIGN OF DEATH

So what is the sign of Jonah? We have already concluded that it will be Jesus' death and resurrection, but is there more to this sign? And how might it relate to finding peace in the middle of a storm? As we have already stated, Jonah did find peace – but only after he had repented through a simple prayer in the belly of the fish.

But even before that, he had to die.

Somehow Jonah knew that the sea would become calm if the sailors threw him overboard. Jonah told his shipmates to pick him up and get on with it. The men expected him to die soon after he hit the water, and Jonah probably thought that too. It is quite possible that Jonah intentionally took steps to sacrifice his life in order to save the lives of others. Perhaps he thought that, if God resurrected him in order to complete his mission, then only God could do that.

That being so, Jonah was willing to die for his shipmates, trusting in a merciful God for the outcome. He wasn't lynched by the sailors and violently thrown overboard; they reluctantly put him into the sea, genuinely fearful that God would punish them for doing so. Jonah freely gave his life to save his fellow passengers. No wonder Jesus compared himself to Jonah.

Jonah was willing to die for a few travellers in danger; Jesus died for the whole of mankind, trusting in his Father to raise him from the dead. When Jesus likened himself to Jonah, he was trying to convey to the teachers of the law that he, the Son of Man, was willing to die for others. Jonah, presumed dead, had lain in the body of a fish. Jesus will die but then be days in the heart of the earth. 'But look what happened to Jonah later,' Jesus is saying to the Pharisees. 'He effectively came back to life, and you will see me, the Messiah, restored to life.'

Sometimes when we experience the storms of life, we ask God for a sign. 'God, show me what you are doing! Please let me know your power and your love. Give me a sign from heaven of your will.' There is nothing wrong with asking for these things, but perhaps there are times when God is calling us to be willing to die just like Jonah was willing to die. When we ask God to give us signs like the ones formed in our imaginations, are we willing to listen to an invitation to put our plans to death? To die to ambition that is not quite in line with his purposes? To die to a desire that may ultimately do us harm? To kneel before the cross once more and call him Lord again?

## DEATH BY BALLS OF PAPER

I remember a time when my job was coming to an end. I had been working for a church in the UK and my contract was not going to be renewed. I hadn't done anything deserving dismissal, but a new pastor had joined the team and he had similar skills to me. With a limited budget, the church didn't need the both of us.

So, I found myself approaching the end of my time there and pondering my future. I had hoped that this appointment might lead to something else but, as it turned out, it was not leading anywhere. For some time, I had felt an inner tug towards serving the Lord in pastoral ministry. I felt that was a 'call'. For the previous two years or so, I had held the responsibility of steering the church towards an effective evangelistic strategy and had received some theological training. I had imagined the next step would be some sort of leadership training and eventually a church to pastor. That all came crashing down when the current church had no more room for me.

My immediate prospects were not looking good. I reflected on the fact that I had incomplete theological training, only some experience in serving a church in evangelism and very little else that might prove useful in applying for a similar job somewhere else. With nothing on the horizon and equally no job opportunities in my previous career as a schoolteacher, I had no idea of what God was saying.

One day, I sat at my desk a little discouraged and thinking about these things. As I stared blankly at a bookcase on the opposite wall, I noticed a small section of its construction that looked like a cross – a Christian cross. I can't remember where I had heard the phrase, but I felt I should put all my concerns 'at the foot of the cross'.

Grabbing some scrap paper, I started to write down all my needs, all my uncertainties, my family's needs, all my ambitions and all my fears. In fact, anything that was stopping me from quietly trusting God for the days and years ahead. And I realised I needed to die to my plans of becoming a pastor. In fact, I needed to die to all ideas about the future. I needed to re-submit my life to the one who made me and saved me. If he wanted me to serve him in the way I had hoped, I'd have to stop worrying about it. He would make it happen in his way and in his time.

I wrote it all down on several pieces of paper and scrunched up each one in turn. Every ball of paper was placed at the foot of the cross, accompanied by a prayer of re-commitment. 'Lord, the future is yours. I die to my own plans and trust you for yours.' I finally found some peace that God had the future in his hands.

## DEATH AND RESURRECTION

Death and resurrection is a common theme in the Bible. In Genesis, Abraham was instructed by God to sacrifice his son, Isaac. When God could see he was willing to go through with it, he stopped him and provided a ram instead. One might argue that Isaac had a near-death experience and a sort of resurrection.

Joesph was sold into slavery and presumed dead by his father. Years later, his discovery in Egypt as second only to Pharaoh paints another picture of a type of resurrection to new life. Elijah raised a widow's son[121], and Elisha raised the Shunammite woman's son.[122] Jesus commanded Lazarus, dead for four days, to return to life.[123]

When Paul wrote about believers being 'buried' with Christ through baptism, he talked about us being baptised into his death.[124] We die to our own lives when we believe in his sacrifice on the cross. When we repent of sins and receive his forgiveness, we relinquish control of our lives. We give our lives to him. "You are not your own; you were bought at a price."[125] He owns us now. But the promise is resurrection.

"Just as Christ was raised from the dead through the glory of the Father, we too may live a new life."[126]

When we die, Jesus promises resurrection. That promise is for the end of our lives, but I also believe it is a principle for living our lives and walking with God while still on the earth. From time to time, God gives us the opportunity to ask: am I willing to die to my own ambitions and plans and, instead, trust him to lead me into his?

It wasn't long after my ball-scrunching prayer that Sue and I sensed the Lord leading us to move to Western Australia. Now, twenty years later I can see that his call to serve in pastoral ministry could only have happened over here in this country. I needed to die in order to be put in the right place.

---

[121] 1 Kings 17:17–24
[122] 2 Kings 4:32–37
[123] John 11:1–44
[124] Romans 6:3–4
[125] 1 Corinthians 6:19–20
[126] Romans 6:4

## Summary

- The Pharisees wanted Jesus to give them a sign.
- The only sign he would give them was the sign of Jonah: death and resurrection.
- When Jonah was swallowed by the fish he effectively died but he was also *willing* to die.
- Sometimes when we lack peace during life's storms, the Lord may be calling us to die to our plans and ambitions and recommit our lives to him.

## Key takeaway

The sign of Jonah is death and resurrection. When the storms of life strike, take it as an opportunity to die, to re-submit your life to him.

# CHAPTER 10

# *Greater than Jonah*

"The men of Nineveh will stand up at the judgment with this generation and condemn it; for they repented at the preaching of Jonah, and now something greater than Jonah is here."[127]

Although some translations read 'some*one*' instead of 'some*thing*' (greater than Jonah is here), and others like the New King James Version avoid the issue by saying 'a greater than Jonah is here', it is intriguing to note that Jesus may well be saying a lot more than just some *one*. He is, without doubt, greater than Jonah in a multitude of ways but there is some *thing* that is greater than Jonah too.

One suggestion is that Jesus is talking about his mission. The thing that is greater than Jonah is the mission of Jesus. The mission of Jesus is superior to the mission of Jonah.

## READING JONAH IN THE LIGHT OF JESUS

Jonah was called to go to the Ninevites. Nineveh was an ancient city in Upper Mesopotamia, located in the now modern-day city of Mosul in

---

127 Matthew 12:41

Northern Iraq. Archaeologists tell us that for several decades it was probably the largest city in the world at that time. According to the book of Jonah, it took three days to walk from one end to the other.

In its heyday, Nineveh was the flourishing capital city of Assyria during the time of Judah's King Hezekiah and the prophet Isaiah. The prophet Nahum spoke many denunciations against Nineveh, mostly for her wickedness and cruelty.

> Woe to the city of blood,
> full of lies,
> full of plunder,
> never without victims!
> The crack of whips,
> the clatter of wheels,
> galloping horses
> and jolting chariots!
> Charging cavalry,
> flashing swords
> and glittering spears!
> Many casualties,
> piles of dead,
> bodies without number,
> people stumbling over the corpses.[128]

Jonah came from a town called Gath Hepher in northern Israel.[129] Located in the tribal territory of Zebulun, it was likely a small town or even just a village nestled in the surrounding rural landscape. Jonah was called to leave the quiet calm of country life and step into a large, bustling, not-to-

---

[128] Nahum 3:1–3
[129] Mentioned in 2 Kings 14:25

mention savage city. His first instinct was to run, and we can perhaps have some sympathy for him.

Jonah knew God and was already known as a prophet in Israel. He had a recognised ministry and a position in Jewish society. But the call to relinquish all that, to face terrible danger, fear and loneliness, with a strong likelihood of an early grave among a brutal people in Assyria's vast capital city was too much for him.

Jonah was clearly not Jesus, who:

> …made himself nothing
> by taking the very nature of a servant,
> being made in human likeness.
> And being found in appearance as a man,
> he humbled himself
> by becoming obedient to death…[130]

Was Jonah willing to die for God's purposes in the same way Jesus was? Clearly not at the beginning of the story. However, eventually (as we have previously noted), when the troubled sailors asked him what they should do while facing the terrible storm, he replied, "Pick me up and throw me into the sea, and it will become calm. I know that it is my fault that this great storm has come upon you."[131] At this point he does seem to have reached a point of sacrificing himself for others.

He was willing to die, but only after he could see God had caught up with him and that those around him were in great danger. He was willing to die, but only when cornered. This is not the same as Jesus who 'humbled himself by becoming obedient to death'.

---

[130] Philippians 2:7–8
[131] Jonah 1:12

Jonah eventually made the trip to Nineveh and, after a day's journey into the heart of the city, he started preaching. He had just one message: "Forty more days and Nineveh will be overthrown."[132] The word 'revival' probably underestimates the effect of his words. We are told that literally everybody, young and old, fasted and repented. Even the king "rose from his throne, took off his royal robes, covered himself with sackcloth and sat down in the dust."[133]

Everything Jonah must have feared as he approached the Assyrian capital did not come to pass. God spared him and protected him. He faced no shame and no suffering.

On the other hand, Jesus would have known what lay ahead as he left his Father's side. He would have been very familiar with what was prophesied in the book of Isaiah. Jesus as the Servant will be despised and rejected, he will suffer and be familiar with pain.[134]

Jonah was not asked to suffer and die. He only feared those as possibilities and so he ran. But Jesus was called to suffer and die, and he embraced the Father's will. He went to the cross without resistance. Without doubt, Jesus is one greater than Jonah.

## SOME*THING* GREATER THAN JONAH IS HERE

Jews in Jesus' day would have held Jonah in high regard. He was a legitimate prophet, having successfully relayed God's message to the people of Nineveh. The inclusion of his story among the twelve minor prophets in the Hebrew holy scriptures is testimony to that fact. Even Jonah's reluctance to accept God's mercy on the Ninevites (which is recorded in Jonah

---

[132] Jonah 3:4
[133] Jonah 3:6
[134] Isaiah 53:3

4:1–3) might have resonated with some Jewish thinkers who struggled with the concept that God's love extends to other nations.

So for Jesus to announce to the Pharisees and teachers of the law that something greater than Jonah stands before them was a brave thing to do. But very necessary. Only later might they fully understand the impact of his claim.

Jonah went from a peaceful village to a dangerous and sinful city – reluctantly. Jesus left his Father's side to a world under the control of the evil one – willingly. Jonah submitted to the inevitability of death in the open sea (still preferable perhaps to torture and death by the hands of the Ninevites). Jesus was willing to die a shameful and painful death.

That's some *one*, but what about some *thing* – the mission?

Jonah's mission was to go to one city and "preach against it"[135] for just that moment in time. Jesus came to earth to "seek and save the lost"[136] for all eternity. Jonah was just one man. Jesus called disciples, who made more disciples, who made even more disciples until the presence of Christ is felt in every nation on Earth today.

The mission of the Son of God, compared to that of the minor prophet was far bigger and far wider. It touched and has touched infinitely more people, with lasting impact up to the present day. And when Jesus told the Pharisees that something greater than Jonah is here, he could probably see it unfolding in his mind's eye. The writer of Hebrews reminds us that it was because of, "for the joy set before him he endured the cross."[137]

---

[135] Jonah 1:1
[136] Luke 19:10
[137] Hebrews 12:2

## PEACE IN THE MIDST OF MISSION

Jesus knew where he was going. He knew the Father's love, protection and guidance and so it shouldn't surprise us that he found peace while lives were being threatened by a freak storm on Lake Galilee. He wasn't worried by it, and he could even grab a bit of sleep in the middle of it while others lost their cool around him.

We have speculated reasons for this. On that day, Jesus knew the direction the Father wanted them to go so he had faith they would arrive safely. He knew of his much bigger mission to the cross and resurrection from the dead. He was also aware of the authority he had over the winds and waves.

Another possible reason is that Jesus saw a teaching moment in front of him where the disciples might learn more about trust. I sometimes imagine him deliberately letting the storm rage for a while so that the disciples would be forced to face his question, "Where is your faith?" And although Jesus knew things were going to be ok, his other purpose for taking them out of their comfort zone might have been to get their minds thinking around who he really was – his divine identity. To push them to ask the question, "Who is this?"

And if they could work out the answers to both of those questions, they might find that place of quietness and trust for the mission that lay ahead of them, which Jesus will make clear just before his ascension: "...go and make disciples of all nations, baptizing them in the name of the Father and of the Son and of the Holy Spirit, and teaching them to obey everything I have commanded you. And surely, I am with you always, to the very end of the age."[138]

---

[138] Matthew 28:19–20

This leads us again to the personal question about how we might find peace in the middle of our storms today. Maybe a sense of mission is the key.

## WHY ARE YOU HERE?

I was asked this question some years ago by a counsellor after I stepped through the door of his consulting room and sat down. I had experienced some unexpected symptoms of stress to the point that I felt I should talk to my GP.

My doctor, a lovely Christian man who has taken care of me for over twenty years, listened patiently while I talked to him about feelings of anxiety, loss of sleep and a general lack of peace. We agreed that I was likely experiencing some sort of mild 'burn-out', a condition that is sadly common in today's world, particularly among those in ministry. He suggested I schedule several sessions with a counsellor.

So, when my counsellor asked me why I had made the appointment with him, it was fairly easy to answer. I wanted to get better. I wanted to survive the rigours of ministry into the long term, so I needed some help in coping with the pressures I was feeling as well as developing some strategies to help avoid a repeat of what I was going through then.

That wasn't easy to achieve, but years later I can testify to some level of peace as a result of good counsel around the topic of effective self- care.

## WHAT IS YOUR MISSION?

But the question, 'Why are you here?' is a much bigger one if we step back and take a panoramic view of life in general. We have already said that Jesus knew his purpose for coming to earth. He came to seek and save the lost, endure the cross, be raised from the dead and then catapult the church into existence through disciples making disciples making disciples.

It is not hard to articulate Christ's mission on earth and it is not a stretch therefore to link it with characteristics we see displayed in his life: a strong sense of purpose, joy and of course peace during the stressful times. Jesus knew his mission and was therefore at peace when things seemed to get in the way.

Can we know our mission to the same degree? And can we experience the same level of peace when we know our mission?

I believe we can.

If you are a Christian, a follower of Jesus, you are part of a body of people, belonging to Jesus. You are part of the 'body of Christ'[139] and collectively we have a clear call. As Peter wrote, "…you are a chosen people, a royal priesthood, a holy nation, God's special possession, that you may declare the praises of him who called you out of darkness into his wonderful light. Once you were not a people, but now you are the people of God; once you had not received mercy, but now you have received mercy."[140]

Together we have the awesome privilege of declaring the truth and love of Jesus to the world around us. We have a voice to be heard and a message to share. We are chosen and have been made holy, in order that we might speak words of salvation and hope to those in darkness. We are the people of God, receivers of his mercy, offering that same mercy to the rest of the planet.

We are then further called to turn those who listen into more disciples.

That's our mission, but it is easy to miss this as our most important and principal call. Our reason for being alive. We congregate in local expressions around the world to shine a light. At least, that should be the reason.

---

[139] 1 Corinthians 12:27
[140] 1 Peter 2:9–10

Churches are not clubs that meet just to satisfy our own needs. As someone once said, 'The local church is the only organisation that exists primarily for the benefit of its non-members.'[141]

In my experience, churches that understand this have an undefinable joy in their gatherings. They know why they are meeting together, why they serve and why they sacrifice. It's all about doing this for a greater cause – for the good of the world and ultimately for Jesus himself. For his glory. Then, when the storms hit (and they do, because we live in the middle of a spiritual battle), it is possible to collectively find his peace because we know why we are here and what we are called to do.

However, not everybody finds it.

## THE LONE BELIEVER

The idea of not being actively involved in a local church would have been a foreign concept to Christians working out their faith in first century Israel and beyond. If you were a born-again follower of Jesus, you were part of the community of faith, working and serving together for the extension of his kingdom. If there were arguments or tensions, people worked them out. Or tried to. Even when it was messy. Especially when it was messy. One look at the Corinthian church is a case in point.

But today, there is a growing phenomenon in many parts of the world where believers have cut ties with a local congregation. They are more comfortable working out their faith on their own or with just one or two others because of pain or frustration experienced in being part of a local assembly.

I am not referring to occasions where ill health keeps a person at home or situations where the persecution of Christians is rife. I am talking about

---

[141] The is usually attributed to Archbishop William Temple

times where hurts or offences drive a person away from regular Christian fellowship. Or when we lose the vision or hope of what the church is meant to be.

This is one of the saddest observations about the modern church because if one path to peace during life's storms is found through belonging and a joint sense of purpose with other believers, many people are missing out. The lone believer who even for understandable reasons chooses to separate him or herself from regular life with other brothers and sisters in Christ, will have less resources available when the storms come.

Christians are not designed to operate on their own. When the Apostle Paul embarked on his missionary journeys he always sought to work with others in a team. On the rare occasion that wasn't possible, his mental health suffered.

Arriving in Corinth, not long after a harrowing experience in Thessalonica[142], God had reason to comfort Paul with the words, "Do not be afraid; keep on speaking, do not be silent. For I am with you, and no one is going to attack and harm you, because I have many people in this city."[143] Paul's own recollection of the same time had him reflecting with the words, "I came to you in weakness with great fear and trembling."[144] It is not good for Christians to face storms alone.

## PULLING IT ALL TOGETHER

Scripture reveals an undeniable link between the Old Testament prophet, Jonah, and Jesus. Jesus claimed that something about him was greater than Jonah. As the incarnate Son of God, sent by the Father to come to our

---

[142] See Acts 17:5–9
[143] Acts 18:9–10
[144] 1 Corinthians 2:3

planet, he was vastly superior in his obedient humility to fulfil the task set before him. And his mission was greater. Not only because the world contained many more people than one city, Nineveh, but because his message and sacrifice was for all people through all time and all places since then.

Jesus foretold his death and resurrection by describing what was to come as a sign of Jonah. Just as the prophet appeared to die after being thrown in the sea and swallowed by a fish but then found to be alive as the same fish vomited him onto a beach, Jesus predicted he would actually die but be restored to life a couple of days later.

The connections between the two don't end there, however. Both are found at the centre of a story where a storm is miraculously calmed. And as we examine both accounts, we find they speak to us about how we might face our own storms with faith.

The way Jesus handled a stressful and threatening situation that day on Lake Galilee was superior to Jonah's position in similar circumstances. Jonah found a level of peace by repenting of his disobedience and receiving a restored relationship with God, but Jesus demonstrated a whole new level of peace through purpose and relationship with God that even crossed into the realm of the supernatural.

It is not difficult to notice even by a cursory read of the gospels that Jesus was constantly in the process of teaching his disciples faith. While they were trying to figure out who he was, he did everything he could to help them put their trust in him and in the Father.

Peace through life's struggles had always been possible through the teachings of the Old Testament. But now, Jesus was saying, "I am with you." He was literally in the boat with them, despite the wind and waves threatening to end them.

So as we pull these different thoughts together, the great news is that we can live in the good of Christ's mission on earth today. Through the church and through the power of the Holy Spirit. Peace in the middle of life's storms is possible as we apply the teachings of God's Word to our lives, as we work them out within the overall plan of his mission, and as we serve in community with other brothers and sisters in Christ.

## Summary

- When Jesus said that something greater than Jonah is here, it is likely he was talking about his mission.
- Jesus wants us to know our mission, and that is best found in the context of fellowship with other believers.
- As Christians, we are not meant to exist in isolation.

## Key takeaway

When the storms of life strike, face them in the context of his wider mission, and in community with other believers.